PRAYER AND CONTEMPLATION

PRAYER AND CONTEMPLATION

an invitation to discover

by

MARK GIBBARD

Society of St John the Evangelist, Oxford

M

MOWBRAYS
LONDON & OXFORD

ISBN 0 264 62423

First published 1976
by A. R. Mowbray & Co Ltd
The Alden Press, Osney Mead
Oxford OX2 0EG

Text set in 10/12 pt Baskerville
and printed in Great Britain
by Richard Clay (The Chaucer Press), Ltd,
Bungay Suffolk

Contents

Preface

THE world is full of searchers. We are all, or nearly all, searching because we are not content with things—or with ourselves—as they are. In politics, in society and in personal relationships there is a search for fresh openness. And with this search comes often an inner seeking—so rife, so various—for some kind of contemplative living and praying.

Recently I was staying at a secular university, where various small groups in turn use the ecumenical chaplaincy. The only time it has been packed—and then, to overflowing—was when two Tibetan monks came. This was not only the lure of the east, I think, but more a quest for contemplative experience. Everywhere meditation courses are springing up. The same sort of searching, with its obverse, a determination to change society, I have found at Taizé and among the Focolari. It partly motivates the charismatic movement. Indeed, wherever I go, I find groups of people meeting to pray and to explore the wider horizons of contemplation.

I should like to invite you to join in this great search. You don't have *first* to solve your problems about God, the world and yourself. They are often solved on the way. I know them well; I've been an agnostic and have known recurring patches of doubt and obscurity. You can start from just where you are, whatever your ideas and experience.

I am a searcher myself, grateful for the help and encouragement of many friends and writers. And how I need that help still! Then let us start *together* and I will try to keep in mind the practical purpose of what I have to say.

Oxford 1976

MARK GIBBARD

I

FINDING OUR WAY

*Every human being is on the road towards be-
coming his own true self.*

JOHN HEIJKE

CONTEMPLATION and prayer are the blossoming of our
real selves, I think, yours and mine. Two phrases often
rise spontaneously to our lips—at least they do for me—
when we let ourselves be ourselves with other people:
'How marvellous!' and 'I'd love to help.' They well up
from a twofold need deep in our human nature as men
and women.

With this sense of marvel goes often the desire to
open ourselves to *receive* some of this wonder into our
hearts. And with the desire to help there is usually the
readiness to *give* ourselves to others. In friendship and
love this receiving and giving are both fundamental.
They are almost as natural as breathing. Unfortunately
they are much more easily stifled.

As we come to believe in God, perhaps gradually—
and in God who is love—our sense of marvel grows into
a simple, receptive contemplation of God in nature and
in *his self-disclosure*. And similarly our desire to give
and help expresses itself then not only in service to
others, but it also grows *pari passu* into prayer, particularly into intercession.

This need of ours both to receive and to give, de-

9

veloping this way into contemplation and prayer, will be the theme running all through this book. And we shall see that contemplation, contrary to what many people think, has a kind of priority over the commoner forms of prayer, such as intercession, just as the sense of natural wonder can often kindle the desire to give yourself to serve. Marvel is prior to inspired action; and contemplation to deep intercession.

This contemplation is new to me, yet strangely not new. The other day I was emptying some old files. I'm a bit of a hoarder. I came across some round, boyish handwriting I hadn't seen for years. I can't remember writing it or think how I came to write it:

> Show me, Lord, how to be quiet, to know and love thee:
> then I can pray and be of use in the world.

The words about being quiet, knowing and loving surprise me most. I hadn't been particularly religious. Other things meant more to me. My prayers, such as they were, like many boys' prayers, were aimed at getting God to do something for me and other people. Yet gladly I can still use those same words today, but with one essential addition now:

> Show me, Lord, how to be quiet, to *receive* thy love for me;
> to get to know and love thee, to pray and be of use in the world.

I couldn't help thinking of those lines of T. S. Eliot, with those haunting last four words:

> We shall not cease from exploration.
> And the end of all our exploring

Will be to arrive where we started
And know the place for the first time.

The Beginning of Contemplation

As perhaps some will look at this book who are vague about their belief in God, let us glance first for a moment at *natural forms of contemplation*. They come often from experiences of beauty and of love. When, for instance, you watch, you contemplate, the white crest of a wave falling down with a final shudder on wet sand, your mind relaxes, expands, is still and is refreshed. Or when you realise you are loved and you love, you cannot find words to hold this mystery; you rest silently, content and renewed. In each experience you perceive and you receive something. There are quite other happenings of this kind: a friend told me that the sight of a bitch caring for her puppies 'turned him on'. Very many people have these experiences—little metamorphoses—unaware that they can be the beginning of a kind of natural contemplation. We probably need to find out how to recognise, to prolong and sustain them. So some whose beliefs are vague can *already* contemplate. And perhaps this contemplation may itself help the haze to lift.

When we begin to be aware of God, or as we grow to know him more deeply, what we receive in *religious contemplation* is more profound and intimate. For God is like the air we breathe, always around us and within us, sustaining us. I do not mean that he is impersonal like the air. He is personal, not as you and I are, but in a much more wonderful way. He can and does disclose himself, and is able—incredible as it may seem to some of us now—to build up real personal relationships with us.

11

At the beginning of our search, however, we should not aim too high or impose on ourselves times for contemplation and prayer which are too long. Rather we should find out how our interest and our appetite can grow. For prayer, Teilhard de Chardin said, should not be felt as an additional burden to life, but rather should be 'a source of immense power which bestows significance and beauty and a lightness of touch on what we are already doing'.

I am writing about something which strangely enough I've only recently discovered. Yet I half knew it already. I used to think that contemplation was for a spiritual élite. But now I have found that, at least in a simple form, it is an open door for us all. Perhaps you wish to press me to define contemplation. Some writers in the past have given it restricted, technical meanings; and at them we will glimpse later in this book, in chapter 8. I cannot define contemplation, but I will clarify how I intend to use it; and I will be as bold as Humpty Dumpty when he said to Alice: 'When I use a word, it means just what I choose it to mean—neither more nor less.' Contemplation for me is *perceiving receptively*. St John of the Cross said: 'To contemplate is to receive.' But we perceive, we contemplate not only through our eyes. Although this word is derived from *contemplari*, to gaze at, contemplation can come also, for instance, through hearing poetry read or music and through memory's door.

In specifically *Christian contemplation* it is not so much that we have something to perceive but, rather, Someone to love us. We sense God in creation but even more in his self-disclosure in Jesus. Particularly through Jesus Christ we realise that we are actually loved by God and can with his help respond with our love. This experience is a *gift* that comes to us in many different and often unexpected ways. Through this receiving love and responding with love we grow more and more into those real, mature men and women God wishes us to be—those men and women he desires to use in the transformation of the world.

Lots of people today are discovering or re-discovering this simple, receptive contemplation. René Voillaume, founder of contemplative fraternities in the world, has written: 'Every human being has within him, however much or little he may be aware of it, a contemplative dimension.' I think he is right. Contemplation has been called *the* prayer for busy, unhurried people! Many modern young people seem to have a special affinity for it. René Voillaume notices how they are 'at ease in the setting of solitude and prayer, stripped of all un-essentials'. But this does not make them remote from or indifferent to the world. They are searching for authentic commitment as well as authentic prayer. As René Voillaume continues: 'The contemplation of God, far from cutting us off from others, alone allows us to love them in the manner in which God loves them.'

Contemplation and Transformation

I am convinced, and seem to have guessed as a boy, that our contemplation and our being of real use in the world are inseparable. Indeed, contemplative praying should lead to the transformation of the world. So I welcome warmly this renewal of contemplation, but *only* as long as it does not mean a running away from the political and social problems around us. Frère Roger spoke about this danger to thirty-five thousand young people, camping at Taizé for the 1974 session of their Council of Youth. He called upon them to engage in the struggle to free men everywhere from oppression. Through contemplation they would receive the necessary strength from God; and also, equally important, contemplation would save them from arrogantly imposing their ideas on others. *Lutte et Contemplation,* struggle and contemplation, both he called 'the two poles between which we are to situate our whole existence'.

This is what the pattern prayer which Jesus gave us has always been saying, perhaps unnoticed by us. Its pivot is 'They kingdom come'; and all the words following are the spelling out of the implications of those three words. But very significantly *before* we pray—and work—for the kingdom, our Lord turns our hearts and minds first to contemplate God himself, disclosed as our Father.

These two poles of struggle and contemplation we see activating the life of Mother Teresa today. With only five rupees in her pocket, she went to live among the poorest of the poor in the slums of sweltering Calcutta. She began by caring for a few abandoned children. She next made out of a deserted Hindu temple a shelter where the dying could die, surrounded by love. Scores of helpers were drawn as by a magnet to share in her life of extreme poverty and joyful love. Quickly her work spread to other Indian towns, to Latin America, to a Jordanian refugee camp and to hate-pocked Belfast. Her secret is in her words—and by 'meditation' she means, I think, our simple form of contemplation: 'The more we receive in silent prayer, the more we can give in our active life. Love to pray, feel often during the day the need to pray. Love is a fruit in season at all times. Everyone can receive this love through meditation, the spirit of prayer and sacrifice, by an intense inner life.'

Our Need to Explore

But do we have to go to Taizé or Calcutta to find out that prayer and contemplation are something that we need continually to explore? Some seem to think that they can be learnt once and for all, like a sketch-map of Boston or Liverpool. A friend of mine had had a serious illness and was invited by a retired army officer and his wife to spend his convalescence in their cottage. The couple were admired by everyone and were regular supporters of the village church. Their guest thought he would like to give them a small 'thank you' present. He chose that charming yet profound book—with a contemplative flavour about it—*How to Pray*, by Père Grou. Hardly had my friend gone, when his host exploded to his wife: 'What a cheek! To give us at our age a book on how to pray. I've prayed all my life. I learned it at my mother's knee.'

Many think like him, but would express themselves less strongly. Some plod on, bedevilled by routine. Others, all interest dead, gradually drop praying entirely or else deliberately reject it. Yet close at hand, if only they knew it, are new ways of prayer and contemplation, like half-hidden paths branching off from the main beaten track through a forest—tiny, fascinating paths which eventually open up into pools of sunlight. One sad result of our blinkered attitudes to prayer is that some who are searching for a new, authentic way, may never think of looking for help and encouragement from Christians and their churches.

Don't misunderstand me. I don't mean that prayer is a technique that you can find in a book. Yet prayer, though natural, has to be learned. Isn't it the same with friendship, love and many other things? Some book-knowledge may even be quite useful, especially at the beginning. There are plenty of books, for example, about the technique of marriage and of bringing up children; and they sell well. But few couples will follow these books mechanically. They take from them what seems suitable, learn from experience and discover their own way. It is a multiple learning. And so with contemplation and prayer.

Some people—I don't say all—*need* to strike out from time to time into new paths of prayer. The idea came to me very clearly during a recent visit to Australia, while I was chairing a discussion at Sydney, only a few miles from Botany Bay. And I was thinking of the first British settlers who landed there. The new country looked to them not so very different from England. So they made replicas of all they had known at home—farms, barns, coffee-houses and even a conventional English church. They thought they knew their new home. But what lay to the west of their narrow coastal strip beyond those blue hills of the Great Dividing Range? They had no idea. They knew nothing either of the vast deserts or of the priceless hidden deposits of mineral wealth.

So our prayers should not be rehashes. We should stretch our imagination and our muscles. We shall probably have some arid patches to cross, it may sometimes be hard going. But it will be well worth while. For there will be also immense spiritual treasures of love and understanding ready for us to unearth—and then to share with others to their great joy.

To invite you to strike out and explore for yourself is largely why I am writing this book. *But your reading is not journeying*. We each need to make our own exploration, not resting content with our own Botany Bay. And the journey will be rather different for each one of us. We each have our own temperament, we each make our own discoveries. We do not put pressure on others to follow our own particular track. But that great and mysterious hinterland is for us *all*—I am in on this as well as you—and its exploration is, in a real and timeless sense, a joint one. Sometimes our paths cross; sometimes, even when we feel alone, we know there are and have been lots of others on the same track. What a motley crowd we are, and rightly so!

How much we can be helped and encouraged by reading the memoirs and letters of those earlier searchers. If they warn us of impassable thickets, we had better listen to them—and also if they tell of welcome water-holes in parched country. But we always need to try to go behind their written words to what it felt like for them—the thrill of setting out on new stages of the journey, the relief at dangers circumvented, the ache of weary limbs after a long tramp, and the joy of new discoveries, new lights, new colours, new distant views.

Though we may learn much from their experiences of contemplation and prayer, again we do not imitate. For many of them lived under different social conditions from ours, nor had they some of the insights which we have into the depths of human personality. In effect they knew nothing of modern psychology or sociology, even though we may feel that these sciences are by no means infallible guides.

Guides

But what about guides for the journey? Yes, guides,

but not instructors, I think. Even so, some of us are at first understandably shy of asking advice on such personal matters as our own prayers. We might feel more at home discussing with friends a particular article or book about prayer. But notice, won't you, not only what is said but who says it. Don't take everything at its face value. Some people speak with enthusiasm but without much experience; others, with experience, have lost adventurousness of spirit. We may learn a good deal by discussion. But before long we may discover we need a personal helper—'a guide, philosopher and friend'. A priest or minister might seem an obvious choice; he is, after all, professionally trained for this work. Many lay people also have proved themselves perceptive guides. Though letters of advice can be a help, really you need personal contact, like consulting your doctor. So availability is important.

We should not expect too much detailed guidance from these advisers. That is why I hesitate to use the traditional name 'spiritual director'. Yet some of these old guides were wise as well as precise, and their letters are among the most helpful we could have. In the sixteenth century, a Mme de Chantal unfortunately put herself under the guidance of one very exacting director. This caused great trouble to herself and her household. A little later she met Francis de Sales, the Bishop of Geneva, one of the most discerning of spiritual guides of all ages, and after some hesitation transferred herself to his care—with entirely happy results. A member of her household wrote: 'Madame's first director only made her pray three times a day, and we were all put out by it; but *Monseigneur de Genève* makes her pray all day long, and it doesn't worry anyone.' Another guide of that same period, Father Augustine Baker, used to say: 'The spiritual guide is not to teach his own way, but to instruct others how they may themselves find out the way proper for them.' Reading, listening, counselling, we need to be judicious.

Prayer in the Spirit

For Christians the principal guide is the Spirit of God within us. That can be made to sound too *simpliste*. Let me try to explain. In our search we shall again and again meet Jesus in the New Testament, in present experience and in the world of today. Jesus shows us a God who is *always* near. And there was something very special in the way Jesus himself prayed. The disciples, as devout Jews, had been praying all their lives; yet they asked him eargerly: 'Lord, teach us to pray.' They sensed something new about his praying and indeed about his whole living. What was it? His certainty of his immediate and complete dependence on God, I think. This confidence is enshrined in a single word—in his Aramaic mother-tongue, *Abba*—the word of mature, wondering, affectionate trust in God as his Father. Jesus made the word 'prayer' as well as the word 'love' new words for us.

And all that Jesus in his love has done for us was done in order to make *us* able to participate in his sonship, and so really to say *Abba* with that very same wondering, loving confidence. This we could never have done by ourselves, however hard we tried. We can only authentically say *Abba*, when the Spirit of God directs our hearts. For God is not only Lord above, he is also the Spirit *in* our hearts. The early Christians so treasured this intimate word *Abba*, that even when they translated Jesus' other words into their Greek, they kept this precious Aramaic word untranslated.

'God has sent the Spirit of his Son into our hearts, through whom we can say *Abba*, Father.' This is the secret of our prayer, the apostle Paul said—and of our daily life also. For, if through prayer we become so sure of God, we shall not be very anxious about what is going to meet us round the next corner. Prayer changes the whole style of our lives.

I have just described what we mean by praying in the Spirit. Not only what is sometimes now called 'charismatic prayer' but *all* genuine prayer is praying in the Spirit, whether we are praying alone or with friends or in the worship of the Church. It is the Spirit of God helping us to pray.

But how can we be sure, you may ask, whether we are really praying in the Spirit? Might we possibly be deluding ourselves? Let us try not to ask this question in too anxious a way. When people are in love, they also sometimes ask: 'Is this only an infatuation?' Occasionally it is, but far more often it is love in one of its many real forms.

There are outward criteria. If our prayer is making us more loving, more ready, for instance, to try to understand 'difficult' people—even if this change is taking place in us rather slowly—this is a good sign that our prayer is on the right track. If we have a wise guide to go to, he out of his wider experience may help us to avoid pitfalls, and so give us assurance.

Further, if we wish to pray about some particular and important matter, such as changing our job, then besides praying, we should weigh up the 'pros and cons' dispassionately. We should ask advice of those who know us personally and also of those who can look at the situation with knowledge and detachment. And our prayer should be, I think, not 'Lord, I wish to do this' but rather 'Lord, I am grateful for all that I owe you; give me light to see how I with my particular limitations and gifts can best express in my service my gratitude to you.' God gives light not usually in a lightning flash, but like the gradual dawning of the day. But let us not make major decisions on the basis of our own prayers alone.

These safeguards are important, but then let us have confidence and go on with joy seeking our way. For the New Testament discloses to us that God *is* love. It does not just say 'God loves', as if loving were one of the many things God does. The saying 'God is love' does not imply softness. It means when God creates, when he trains us, when he disciplines us, it is *always* because he loves us. He loves far more deeply than we love him. The father in Jesus' parable did not wait for his returning son to knock at the door: he ran down the road, welcomed him and embraced him. This is how God loves us and elicits our response in prayer. It may seem almost incredibly wonderful. But this is what Jesus has disclosed.

Perhaps we could pause now, dwell a moment or two on this *fact* of God's love and try to put into words our hopes and needs for the journey. Words like the following may help us trustfully to make a start:

We wish to explore this continent of prayer and contemplation;
    Help us to discover the paths you intend for us;
    Help us to find and share treasures which meet our needs.
    We need you to guide and strengthen us day by day;

May we on this journey know the Spirit of Jesus
   in our hearts,
So that we can live and pray with love and confidence *Abba*, Father.

2

SPONTANEITY AND PATTERN

He sings each song twice over,
Lest you should think he never could recapture
The first fine careless rapture.

ROBERT BROWNING

SPONTANEITY is the very breath of friendship and love—the surprise present, the unexpected letter, the breathless rush with the impetuous: 'Oh, I must tell you at once.' Yet we can't *live* on the spontaneous. We need also a fairly regular pattern, or we don't know where we are—the planning together, the working together, times together, the regular letters, the phone calls we can count on. And so, I think, with living prayer.

Towards the end of a conference on prayer a businessman said to me: 'I never kneel down to pray at home. I go to church with my family most Sunday mornings, because I think Christians should support one another and praise God together. I also talk to God a good deal during the day—but nobody knows it. I thank him for the signs of his goodness, and for the people I see. And if I have to make important decisions, I really pray a lot.' And then he asked me: 'Will that do? What do you think?' I could only reply, 'Magnificent', and I wasn't pretending, I meant it. Every positive thing he said—and the way he said it—was excellent. I would guess that he was more a man of prayer than some of us whose daily prayers are mere routine. And I am discovering more and more that, unless we speak to God spontaneously while we go about our daily life, as he did—or at least keep looking at things in the clearest light God gives us—then our ordinary prayers are not going to be deep or very effective.

Times of Prayer

Yet what puzzled me was how he managed to keep up his steady praying-throughout-the-day. He must be different from me. I'm sure I couldn't keep it up without regular times for prayer. If two people love each other, they think of one another dozens of times a day. This comes naturally. Their love is a joy and a strength to them both, a deep undercurrent that also makes them more cheerful and helpful, as it flows through their everyday lives. But for this to go on, they know that they must, except in abnormal conditions, *make* times to talk and be alone together. And they want to. When they have to be away from each other, they keep in touch and, even if letters have to be short, they convey more than news alone.

Many have discovered the same thing in prayer. I think of Francis and his little town of Assisi. South of it is the rich plain of Spoleto, with its dozen busy villages, the rumbling of carts, the babble of children's voices, the distant ringing of church bells. Along those twisting roads went Francis, singing the praises of God and sharing his love with others. But I remember, too, turning in the opposite direction and climbing through the beech woods and past grey precipices to the summit of those bare, silent Apennines and to Francis' precious hide-out, Monte La Verna, where he spent hours, days, in contemplation, alone with the Alone. We each need our own Spoleto and our own La Verna.

And above all, wasn't this so with Jesus? Was anyone so involved in the sicknesses, frustrations and sorrows of others? Yet even there he turned for a moment again and again to God, *Abba*, Father. But to sustain these moments he had to go out before dawn to find a quiet spot for prayer; and sometimes after a long day's work, he would spend hours on the hillside, lost in prayer.

I know Francis and Jesus are far beyond us. But they show us clearly our needs as men and women—to share loving service with others in a thousand ways—and to have that love replenished in times of contemplation and prayer. Those times, perhaps short, but authentic, alone with the Lord, are practically indispensable, I believe, if our lives are to be lives of love and service in the world.

But how hard it is for some people to find time— mothers with young children, others with aged, sick relatives, or hard-pressed doctors and social workers. I know this; I've lived with ordinary people in an old, industrial town. But don't let us say too quickly, 'It's impossible.' We might have a shock if for one week we logged the time we frittered away. And it's surprising what we can do, if we want to. For prayer we have to be ready—and, if we can, be glad to be ready—for sacrifices. We do this if we love someone. So let us do what we can; and then be neither anxious nor scrupulous about it. If we occasionally miss our time of prayer, it doesn't matter very much, providing we are trying to build up a rhythm of loving prayer. Even more than our time, what God desires is our hearts.

Regularity of our daily prayers has importance. I

hesitate to say that prayer is like a skill, because prayer is much more like friendship. But Paderewski once said: 'If I stop practising the piano for one day, I notice the difference; if I stop for two days, my family notices the difference; if I stop for three days, my friends notice the difference; and if I stop for a week, the public notices the difference.' This, I believe, is normally true of prayer, certainly of mine: the quality of our love for God and our neighbour deteriorates, if prayer ceases to be genuine and *regular*.

It is not as if a rhythm of prayer is to be imposed on an otherwise chaotic day. Demands on our time vary enormously; but we all, like Wordsworth's earth, have a 'diurnal round': most of our days have a basic pattern, like a piece of music, with its phrases and rhythms, its pauses and 'repeats'—and its codas. If you think of it, life is full of rhythms; we depend on them. They are natural to us. Once alert to the likely pattern of your days, you can find and add that regular beat of prayer that rings true for you.

We are fellow-explorers. What I'll do is to pass on to you other people's experience. I've promised to tell you what I've found useful. It may give you something to think over. I know the pressure of time. I enjoy my life; but it is chock-a-block with writing, speaking, travelling, meeting people. Yet experience has proved that the quality of my work, as of my loving, soon goes sharply down, if I do not make my particular times of daily prayer; only by sticking to them do I manage to get through the day. I cannot speak for anyone else, but I know I need two periods of prayer each day—besides times of corporate prayer required by my vocation as a priest. Sometimes I've been tempted to think this corporate prayer by itself is enough. Experience has proved me wrong. I now agree with Frère Roger of the Taizé community: 'Corporate prayer does not dispense us from personal prayer. The one sustains the other. Let us each day take time to renew our personal intimacy with Jesus.'

What I am going to say about times of prayer will sound more stereotyped than it actually is. That can't be helped. When we talk of the deeper things of life—art, music, friendship—it always sounds too patterned. Personally I need a time, if it is at all possible, early in the day, before the telephone starts to ring, before people start to call on me—a time for receptive, contemplative praying. And I also need a second time—I can't think of a satisfactory word to describe it—to give and to share the joys and the responsibilities of the day with the Lord. Personally I find these two times correspond to those *two basic needs* of our human nature, the receiving and giving of love and trust. The second time comes in the late afternoon or evening. If necessary, I can manage part of it while travelling. The end of the day it quite good for me, but not for everybody. But if I am going to be really late, I try to go to my room for prayer before I go out. If I don't manage this and come home exhausted, I stand for my short time of prayer, so as not to fall asleep. Always a few sincere words is infinitely better than nothing at all—in prayer and in love.

Places of Prayer

Jesus' advice is: 'When you pray, go into a room by yourself, shut the door, and pray to your Father who is there in the secret place.' Then Jesus gives us the reason for this advice. We are, he says, in danger of play-acting in prayer—of thinking at least with a quarter of

27

our mind of what impression we are making on others. Practically all my life I have had a room or a study which I could call my own. I'm fortunate, perhaps I don't realise how fortunate. I like to keep a small table there exclusively for my prayers. Praying by a bed is too conducive to sleep for me. On this table I keep an open bible, a few books for prayer, and a crucifix as a focus for my love and prayer. These small things can be great helps—especially on our more difficult days— like the photograph on your desk of someone you love. The same heart loves those dear to you, and loves God, and draws nearer to him in prayer. Of course we have to watch that photographs, crucifixes and other helps do not become mere superficialities, like the familiar pictures on the wall which we only look at when we dust them.

But Jesus often had no room to himself. It was an age of small and crowded houses; and he was often on the road, and sleeping where he could. He had experience of as difficult conditions—at least for prayer— as many people have today. But he knew he needed solitude for his prayers, so he used to go out to find a quiet corner. If we wish for silence, we can perhaps find it in a silent church, in a quiet library—as I used to when a student—or in a park. Quite unconventional places will do for prayer, if we know we can be undisturbed.

Postures in Prayer

I'm surprised how often I'm asked: 'What position should we take up for prayer?' Perhaps we have a feeling that it helps us to be sincere with God, as it does with our friends, if we express ourselves not only with our words, but with eyes, with our bodies. Smiles and gestures not only please our friends, but they are also an integral part of ourselves. For while phoning from our homes, we smile, we frown and even thump the table.

Kneeling comes naturally to many of us and, if this is not mere habit, our bodies are then expressing both our feeling of reverence and our sense of dependence on God's love and mercy. But Richard Rolle, one of our English medieval contemplative writers, wrote: 'Sitting, I am most at rest and my heart most upward. I have loved to sit, for thus I loved God more and I remained longer within the comfort of love than if I were walking or standing or kneeling.' And we may find this, as our own prayers become more receptive and contemplative. But we had better avoid those chairs which make us feel drowsy. Ignatius Loyola recommends us first to stand still a few paces away from where we are going to pray and recollect with reverence what we are about to do. I have found that useful. Then he goes on to say that kneeling, prostrating, lying on your back or standing upright are all at different times helpful. We must be sure, he adds, that we are really seeking God and that we are not fidgeting and keeping on changing our position.

And a few words for those who can't sleep well or who wake very early. As people grow older, they probably need less sleep. When we go to bed, though, I think we should go to sleep if we can, perhaps with the help of a little reading. When I was a science student, I used Addison's *Coverley Papers* to put me off to sleep. But if we can't sleep, why not pray? Sometimes a few quiet words of trust will do wonders. Yet night with its stillness has been for many a favourite time for prayer. Jesus prayed before dawn and sometimes through the night. Charles de Foucauld wrote from Beni-Abbès, a Saharan oasis on the frontier of Morocco: 'I think of Jesus' nights of prayer on the mountains. I should like to keep company with him. Night is the time for intimate converse, for loving and intimate conversation with him.' Henry Vaughan wrote too of 'dear night':

> Christ's progress and his prayer time,
> The hours to which high heaven doth chime.

Unfortunately the worry or tenseness which keeps us from sleep often keeps us also from quiet, trustful prayer. Yet it is worth trying to see whether saying by heart some psalm or poem, or slowly reading the bible or some familiar spiritual book—I do not mean study —might not lead us into prayer—perhaps prayer of a simple contemplative kind. This praying in the night or very early in the morning may be a godsend for some whose lives are so packed with responsibilities that they can seldom find much quiet.

Words of Prayer

I am also often asked whether it is better to pray in our own words or to use a book of prayers. We must each discover for ourselves. I myself prefer to pray spontaneously. But often I find myself using words of praise and prayer, which just spring to my mind, from the bible or the worship of the Church.

There is for me, and perhaps for you, another question about how far our prayers should be systematised. Of course I shall want to pray *every day* for those I love and for those for whom I have some close responsibility. But what about others? My prayers, I feel, should spread out to them; and I can't leave this to chance.

My work brings me into close contact with many people. Of course God doesn't need to be reminded of their needs. But I mustn't forget them; I must be ready to help them by my prayers, as I should by a letter and by an act of friendship. With a memory as bad as mine, I have to write down their names. 'Even the best memory', a Chinese proverb says, 'is weaker than the palest ink.' And as there is not time to pray for them all daily, I write down their names and arrange them over the days of the week. But I must never let this become a mere list. Unless I go on caring, unless I love or unless I wish to love, I can't, I think, really pray. I will return to this question in chapter 5.

Prayer and Doubt

But for some people much more serious than the problem of words is the problem of fundamental doubts. They have told me how worried they have been about their doubts. Most of us are reticent about speaking of our own experience. But to do so can sometimes help other men and women. So let me speak of my own experience. In my home and school I had been brought up as a Christian. You will remember that schoolboy prayer of mine. At the university I began by doing natural science, as I had set my mind on being a physicist. Then I thought I had a call to the ministry of the Church. So I switched my studies to theology. Then my troubles began. Within a few months I had lost all faith in God—very upsetting for someone who wanted to be a priest. In my new studies I had been reading some psychology. At that time it appeared to me that psychology had proved that there was no God, that the whole idea of God was a delusion, an image thrown up my unconscious mind, no more a reality than a mirage in the desert. This, I then said to myself, is the end of religion for me.

Luckily I had a friend, a priest, an acute scholar, who proved himself a wonderful guide in many related fields. Among other things he helped me to see that because psychology like other sciences delimits its field of research and confines itself to the human personality, it can only speak about that and it cannot say anything for or against the reality of God himself. Dr Stafford-Clarke has since then written: 'There is nothing in psychology which makes impossible belief in God.'

How many more things I owe to my friend and guide! Endlessly patient with my argumentativeness, he helped me step by step to build up the whole structure of faith from scratch—Why believe in God? Who is Jesus Christ? What about the miracles, and particularly the resurrection of Christ? What about the Spirit and the Church? And is there a life to come? He suggested at the same time that I should try not to give up altogether going to church with my friends, even if I could accept only in a very rarefied, symbolical way the language of the services. He asked me to leave open the possibility that something real was happening in worship, however inadequate the words might be. I thank God for his advice now. Without it I might easily have slipped away from God for ever.

A great man of prayer once wrote: 'The truest faith springs out of really honest doubt.' Many of us in the present climate of disenchantment lose our faith; but when we regain it, it is often as different from our first faith as a man's tested mature love is from the spontaneous love of a child. We 'know the place for the first time'. Sometimes doubts come back to swirl about us again like clouds on the mountainside. They take the heart out of our prayer. How well I know it! But the one thing I have discovered is that we mustn't be afraid, we mustn't lose our heads. We need to deal squarely and patiently with these doubts, as my friend did with mine originally, even when they are not only intellectual. And the decision of faith is never final; it needs constant renewal in every fresh situation. (You may know that I have looked at these problems more systematically in an earlier book, *Dynamic of Love*. I might be able to help you more there.)

Prayer and Emotion

In the life of prayer, as in our human relationships, emotion has an important part to play. But in both it is our whole personality which should be involved. And in both for various reasons emotions sometimes refuse to come. So we must prepare ourselves to keep going ahead sometimes without them.

When this problem arises in a marriage, the partners often seek advice from a marriage guidance counsellor. So if difficulties come in the life of prayer, we should not shrug them off our shoulders and say that it doesn't matter or that nothing can be done about it. There are a number of common causes. You would be wise to consult a guide or adviser—and don't wait too long, or the problem may become much more difficult to clear up. The cause may be that we have let ourselves get into a rut, a dull routine; or perhaps we have let a serious inconsistency gradually creep into our lives. But if after searching, no cause can be found, then for a time we must accept this dried-up feeling calmly and, if we can, cheerfully. This, I know from experience, is often difficult to do. But it may be a necessary stage in the growth —perhaps in the purification—of our real prayer. Great men and women of prayer have had this testing. Dietrich Bonhoeffer, in the darkness of his last years of prison life, wrote: 'The God who is with us is the God who forsakes us. Before God and with God we live without God'; yet he continued praying day by day in his cell.

A very discerning modern spiritual guide, John Dalrymple, gives us a useful warning: 'Many, who approach prayer in search of "spiritual experience", only meet themselves at greater depth. This is not the same as meeting God.' In mature friendship and love we do not seek *primarily* for thrills and 'experiences'. What we really want is to love a particular person truly, and to live in fellowship with him. We do not so much seek joys, but joys come to meet us. So in contemplation and prayer we do not seek for 'experience', but for God himself, whom we are growing to love. Then he will transform us—others will notice this more than we shall—and he will use us to bring his love and joy to our world, which so needs love and joy.

Prayer, like love, needs freshness and also pattern. If you haven't a satisfactory pattern of prayer, could you think it over now and make one, perhaps for a couple of weeks or for a month? Try it provisionally and then decide definitely. And, once adopted, our personal pattern of prayer is never to be regarded as a demanding taskmaster; rather it is a supportive and encouraging friend, whom you have found on your journey.

This is what I have discovered myself.

3

WORDS AND IMAGES

*The language of prayer cannot escape formal-
ism, unless wordless prayer transfigures it for us
into the language of love and wonder.*

PIERRE YVES EMERY

I CAN remember it as if it were yesterday, and what we
talked about. It was a long day's walk in the Cotswolds
with a close friend. We had been students together,
before we were made priests together. As we walked
that day, we began with some lively, serious talk, and
then we spoke and laughed about our time at the
university and our friends there. Just before the sun
set, we climbed Cleeve Hill. At our feet was the green
vale of the Severn, beyond it twenty miles off were the
Malvern hills and further still range after range as far
as the Black Mountains of mid-Wales. We sat down,
tired and content. We didn't move, we didn't say a
word. We felt very close to each other. It was a deep and
shared silence. Our words as friends had built up to that
evening silence, refreshing and re-invigorating.

And in our journey of prayer we come to experiences
of silence, alone with God. Our words of prayer can
help to build up to this wonderful silence. So I am
fascinated to watch how we use words. That's the theme
of this chapter. If you should find it rather abstract, you
could skip it—and perhaps come back to it later.

Words—such as friendship and joy, prayer and contemplation—help us to think for ourselves and to communicate with each other. But how often we have felt our experience, even human experience, has *transcended* words! We know this in poetry, perhaps before we know it in prayer. The poets, like Robert Graves in his lines,

> O love, be fed with apples while you may,
> And feel the sun and go in royal array,

find they have to arrange clusters of words to convey an experience that we can reach out to, but never quite grasp. The poet's words leave us sensing a reality deeper than mere words could ever tell. Yet their strange haunting quality lives on in us.

When we use words to speak about God or to speak to God, we may sometimes have to use them in this strange, paradoxical way. Henry Vaughan, poet and man of prayer, could write that in God is 'a deep but dazzling darkness'.

Am I beginning to be too sophisticated? Am I forgetting Jesus' words about 'becoming as little children'? But if you look up those words in the gospel—and it's often good to look up much-quoted passages from the bible or any other literature—you will see that Jesus is not telling us to be unsophisticated, but not to be pushing ourselves forward for the top places in the kingdom.

When we use words in prayer, we may easily oversimplify prayer; for *prayer is infinitely more wonderful than saying words to God.*

Words—their Value

What a wonderful thing it is, though, to be able to

36

use words! The Greeks used to marvel at man, who alone in creation had the skill of words, and they called him *zoon logon echon*—'the living being that has the word'. Words can be rich and memorable.

In our ordinary lives we read perhaps in a letter, or hear, a few words, a line or two, and remember them for a lifetime:

'*all* those treasures in those few days',
or Earth's crammed with heaven,
And every common bush afire with God.

The scene where the words came to us stays clear as crystal too.

In our lives of prayer and faith, words can be imprinted on our memories with equal clarity. I shall never forget the moment when a biblical verse came home to me with indescribable assurance. It was as I heard read in the old Swiss Synodal Version: *C'est dans le calme et la confiance que sera votre force*—'In quietness and in confidence shall be your strength.' Or again the incredible sense of liberation I felt as I was listening to the English Authorised Version: 'Herein is love, not that we loved God, *but* that he loved us.' From that moment I knew in my heart that I was no longer, as I had thought, under a peremptory command to love God—something, for me, dauntingly discouraging and unachievable; but the real truth was that I, as I was, with all my failings, *was loved by God*, and that he only expected of me to let myself respond to his love. Struck on the anvil of reality, those words never cease to reverberate. You too have perhaps experienced words in this way.

Words—their Limitations

And yet words are so limited, so inadequate. 'Life,' said T. S. Eliot, 'is an inevitable wrestle with words and meanings.' Again in ordinary life it is so. We go, for instance, to a wonderful concert and a friend says: 'Tell me all about it.' How can we say it in words? We can show our friend the programme, perhaps also a couple of appreciations by music critics in the newspapers. These will convey something. But you cannot know *what* the concert was unless you were there yourself. Words alone can't do it. It's the same with the appreciation of natural beauty—shadows chasing one another over the Yorkshire moors, the expanse of sea from a headland at sunset, the fresh beauty of Alpine flowers on the edge of retracting snow—we can't describe them; we say they are 'beyond words'. It's more so in friendship and love. Poets may help us, but even they, like Robert Graves, often convey reality by suggestion far more than by description. And our own inadequate words would not add to, they might even diminish, the reality experienced.

In our experience of prayer and faith, words are even more inadequate. God by his very nature is beyond words. Our relationship with him cannot be contained in words. More people are now aware of all these limitations of language, because it's a problem that has been much studied recently. Facing it, I believe, will in the long run help to deepen our life of prayer and faith. It is no new problem, however bewildering. Back in the fourth century the theologian Hilary, Bishop of Poitiers, knew these difficulties; he wrote: 'We must strain the poor resources of language to express thoughts too great for words. We dare to embody in human terms truths which ought to be hidden in the silent veneration of the heart.' And the fact of the inadequacy of our words does not in any way call in question the reality of God and his love for us—any more than lovers' silence calls in question the reality of their love.

Analogies and Images in the Language of Prayer

Even Jesus could not describe God literally in words. He had to use analogies and verbal images. When he spoke of God as our Father, he couldn't have meant, could he, that God was our father exactly in the sense that our human fathers are fathers, or even that God was precisely like an ideal human father? True, in many senses God is like a father, yet in other senses he is not. This is why Jesus and the New Testament writers used other analogies to complement the father–son analogy. We need to remember this always in our language of prayer.

First, in some respects all analogies and images resemble the reality to which they point, and in other respects they differ from it. That is why we must *never over-press* analogies, as if they were precise descriptions, almost mathematical equations, from which other things could be logically deduced. For one example, in Jesus' teaching another analogy about our relationship to God is the subject–King analogy. But clearly we should not deduce from this that when we come to God in prayer and in worship, we should observe the etiquette of the court of Louis XIV. You could think of many other examples.

Secondly, some of these analogies may appear to be irreconcilable, but they really should be seen as *complementary*. In the New Testament there is such a variety of images that illuminate our relationship with

God—and also implicitly our relationships with one another. Professor Paul Minear in his book, *Images of the Church in the New Testament*, counts ninety-six: sons and Father, subjects and King, friends and Friend, bride and Bridegroom, sheep and Shepherd, branches and Vine, in Christ, in the Spirit, in God.

What a good thing it is that to help us to understand our relationship—or our potential relationship —with God, there are so many images. It seems that at least one will 'click' for each one of us. For in our world today, as we all know, some young people have no 'living' relationship with their fathers, and some married people have no 'living' relationship with their partners. But nearly all of us have been given, at some time or other, some kind of satisfactory personal relationship, in which we have received affection and responded to it. So for a moment think now of the richest relationship *you* have had of that kind. This may give you an analogous experience and a clue through which you can explore even more profoundly the relationship which God wishes to give you in prayer and in life.

Yet remember we should utilise as many of these images as we can. I often think of this when I look with admiration at the medieval spire of the university church in the High Street at Oxford. The detail is so delicate that it is in my opinion best seen not by daylight, but by floodlights, at night. Yet for this purpose one projector is not enough; batteries of them are needed, throwing up beams from all sorts of angles. It seems to me that, if this ineffably beautiful spire could represent our true relationship with God, then these beams of light would correspond to the analogies and images used to illuminate that relationship. The analogies and images are all needed, and from particular angles. It is the interplay of beams which shows us where and how to look. So in our life of prayer we should try to keep all these images in play together.

Thirdly, these images are vitally important, because they are, as Jung has called them, *'transformers of energy'*. They not only help us to think about God; even more they help us to respond to him in prayer and in love. Living images link our reason to our intuition, to our heart and to the deep energy of our unconscious being. They are like the turbines which I have watched changing the roaring energy of the mountain torrents into light and heat for thousands of homes in the valley.

Fourthly, you will notice that most of our biblical analogies and images are *personal* ones. Thus they are our least inadequate way of speaking of our loving relationship with God. But none of these analogies, not even that of speaking to God as a friend, is a literal, prose description of prayer; it is still an analogy, an image—pointing to, inviting us to something *infinitely* more wonderful. We know deep down that God is not merely one more person like ourselves, just a person to talk to, even though a person infinitely great.

For God is not *a* being, but Being: God is not only transcendent above all but also immanent in all—as Paul puts it in the letter to the Ephesians, the 'one God and Father of all, who is over all and through all and *in* all'; or, declaring the same thing at the Areopagus in Athens: '*In* God we live and move, in him we exist.' This does not of course imply, as we have seen, that God is impersonal, less than personal, like the atmosphere, or like a life-force; but rather he is more-than-personal, richer-than-personal. That is why, when we come to God, *Abba*, Father, with all confidence and love, yet *this very intimacy is enfolded in a sense of marvel and wonder*. God delights to build up personal relationships with us. And we, Christians, are convinced—on grounds which I will mention in the next chapter—that God has *disclosed* himself in Jesus to make this personal relationship real for you and me, for all of us.

Let me in passing show how this way of regarding God helps to answer another question I'm often asked —Who should we pray to? Some people find it natural to picture Jesus and to speak to him as a friend; then by all means let them do it. Others find this doesn't help them; don't let them worry, they'll find another way, one equally good for them. Some people find it helps them, without picturing him, to speak to God as Father. Yet others speak particularly to the Spirit. In prayer and in life we are with the One, the One who transcends *all* concepts and all ways of approach. Let us each follow our own *attrait*, what helps us most, for God is beyond all our images, though we must try not to fasten so exclusively on one aspect of truth as to neglect the others.

Fifthly, we should, I think, in the life of prayer, *never throw away* our analogies and images, in order to get down to the 'real thing', as people sometimes say. We should resist the temptation to try to speak of prayer in bald, descriptive prose. Prayer and poetry are nourished by imagery. Deep communion with God through prayer and contemplation frequently comes to us in silence, but notice how often analogies and images with all their inadequacies and paradoxes both express and build up to this communion.

And in our prayer let us remember that God is active,

more active than a lover—praying is like loving and, when you love, something *happens* to you—and so let us ask God to make our analogies and images serve their real but limited purpose, and then leave it all to him:

> Take not, O Lord, our literal sense, but in thy great
> Unspoken speech our halting metaphor translate.

Praying is more than Speaking with God

In our early years of praying we often use many words, as in the first days of a friendship. Perhaps we remember how embarrassed we used to feel at that early stage if the flow of conversation seemed to be drying up. But as we got to know one another better, we didn't have to think what to talk about. And later on we could sometimes be with one another—and very happily with one another—without saying many words. And so it is in prayer. We don't ever need words to give God information. 'Your father knows before you ask him.' But we may need words to 'open up' ourselves to God, as we do to a friend; and that is very necessary, if we are to have a relationship of love with God. St Augustine said: 'God does not wish for our words, but for our hearts'—our hearts to transform them by his love, that he may use us in his transformation of the world—'that God may be all in all.'

Even—may I say—so wonderful a word as *Abba* is not descriptive prose but analogical poetry. What poetry does is to extend the language of our oneness-in-love by hinting at new ways to deepen, to experience and to enjoy it. In prayer and contemplation we say words *around the silence of loving*, like the beams of light playing around the shining spire. Isn't this what we do when we are with someone we love? We enjoy within the silence the joy of being with each other. Even then words may sometimes come spontaneously to our lips. At other times as on that Cotswold walk we use words and plenty of them. But even then beneath the flow of these words we sense—more at some times than at others—the hidden flow between us of wordless confidence, joy and love.

Praying in this way we find is indeed an exploration. Many of the words and images which we use frequently in our prayers have come to us through the great men and women of prayer before us—Isaiah, Jesus himself, the apostle Paul, Francis de Sales, Charles de Foucauld and a multitude of others. We believe that in some sense God himself through them has been giving us these great phrases. So we should regard these words not as ends in themselves, but as signs calling us to explore, to go beyond, always beyond. So in our contemplation and prayer we should go on and on to seek that sparkling water of strength, joy and love which flows to refresh and renew us; and to slake the thirst, only half-recognised, of the people of all nations.

Could you and I in our next time of quiet prayer— even if this is a new experience for us—trace this glittering stream even further on to the *Spring* himself? For behind all our words and images of prayer there is our inborn 'thirst for God, the living God' himself; and this thirst can best be expressed in the wordless language of love and wonder.

4

SETTLING DOWN

God looks to you to be more open.
TEILHARD DE CHARDIN

A JEWISH man of prayer said enigmatically: 'The preparation for prayer sometimes surpasses in spiritual value the prayer itself.' Yet many of us have often just flopped on to our knees and got on at once with our routine prayers. I now regret my own casualness in prayer; but I regret even more—may I say in passing —the casual way in which we have often begun our prayers with children and young people. We must have given the impression that prayer is just 'something else that must be done' like other daily chores. No wonder some young people give up praying.

Long-range Preparation

'What you are before prayer,' said Cassian, who in the fourth century brought the Eastern tradition of Christian prayer into the West, 'that is what you are in prayer.' So real prayer requires serious preparation, long-range and immediate preparation. But don't misunderstand me. Prayer and contemplation do not involve for us turning away from warm human friendships and from our responsibilities in the world. Unfortunately some books—even parts of that classic, *The Imitation of Christ,* by Thomas à Kempis—have given

45

that kind of impression. Consequently Teilhard de Chardin, in his *Milieu Divin*, has to dispel 'the suspicion that our religion makes its followers inhuman' and has to show how 'the love of God and a healthy love of the world' can actually nourish one another.

Our long-range preparation is wholly positive and includes three things. First, we need to keep fresh in our mind what prayer really is. To regard it—as we so easily can—as one more duty, is fatal. Prayer means marvelling at God's love, receiving it, responding to it, being united with it and sharing it in the world— so that we can live contemplatively and constructively. Mother Julian said: 'Prayer oneth thee to God.' So I recommend what I might call 'prayer-renewal' books, like André Louf's *Teach Us to Pray*. To read slowly, outside our times of prayer, that kind of book, keeps our prayer alive.

Secondly, we should read reflectively some books about God and his disclosure of himself in Jesus Christ. Prayer goes dull unless our understanding of God and our wonder at his love are growing, just as our friendships lose their warmth and sometimes peter out, if we are not *growing* in understanding, appreciation and openness to one another. Archbishop Michael Ramsey has written: 'Theology and spirituality cannot be separated; and the study of truth and the lifting up of the soul in prayer go together.'

This kind of reading will also help us face the many difficulties for our faith in the world of today. And we need to prepare ourselves to help others who meet problems. Perhaps the greatest of these is—and always has been—suffering and evil. People ask us how we can, in face of all this, speak of God and God who is love. It is the tragedies of the world and the apparently sense-

46

less suffering of those dear to us that do so much to shake our confidence and discourage us from prayer.

Frankly I have never found a logically satisfying answer to that problem. In the life of faith and prayer, we have to go on undiscouraged with this problem unresolved on our hands. But then in every field of study there are their unsolved problems. Even the physicist, if I understand it correctly, has to hold side by side two apparently conflicting hypotheses about the nature of light, one understanding light as wave motion and the other understanding light as *quanta*, pellets of energy. This unresolved dilemma does not lead him to give up physics—and take to writing novels. So even our graver problem of evil need not make us throw in our hand and give up praying.

But there is another factor. There are times, I grant, when for me life is like the sky covered with these black clouds of evil and suffering. And I can never minimise them or try to explain them away. But then in those clouds I see a glimmer, then a stronger light, then a beam of sunlight. And that is enough to assure me that there is light and love beyond the clouds. That beam is of course the life and the person of Jesus Christ, who discloses God himself to us in a way that nothing else can.

This disclosure is spelt out for us with increasing clarity as we go through the books of the New Testament. It is not a doctrine invented later on. It is all there implied, I believe, in our earliest records. To give only one example from the earliest gospel, St Mark's: Jesus himself in the parable of the workers in the vineyard contrasts his own relationship with God with that of the Hebrew prophets, the most inspired of his predecessors. He is son; the prophets are only servants.

This means that when we look at Jesus we see what God is like. St John's gospel subsequently sharpens this truth, when Christ there says: 'He who has seen me has seen the Father.' When we see in the gospel how Jesus loves, we know how God always loves each of us —in spite of this inexplicable mass of suffering around us.

May I repeat what I said earlier: true love is never weak love. We see that in Jesus' love. The same love that made Jesus speak so tenderly and so discerningly to the prostitute in the Pharisee's house, made him speak those hard, unwelcome plain truths to the Pharisee himself. Jesus' love made him say blunt things to some men—to set them free from their hard, misguided self-confidence. So God has sometimes to shake us and discipline us; it is an essential part of his loving us. But Paul, who himself had a tough life, was convinced that for those who look to God with love, God can in some mysterious way work all things, even hard things, for our good.

Thirdly, to prepare for prayer we learn to forgive others and to love them. Jesus said that if someone on his way to worship at the temple remembered that a brother had a grievance against him, he should first go and make peace with his brother before entering the temple. And that wonderful fourth chapter of the first letter of John tells us that genuine loving of God and loving one another are *inextricably* interwoven.

This can't mean that, unless we're getting on well with other people, we can't really pray. What then does it mean? Jesus, when he talked about loving our neighbours, can't have meant that we should *feel* affectionate towards people who have made life hard for us and for thousands of others. That is impossible. But he means that we should at least ask ourselves: 'What makes them like that?' That attempt to understand is at least the beginning of love—and then, hard work as it is, we must try to be ready to do something for them, if we have an opportunity; and be ready to apologise when we ourselves are at fault. Though if the other person does not respond, we must not feel too depressed; as Paul says in one of his letters: 'If possible, as far as it lies with you, live at peace with all men.'

Neither can we love everyone in the same way. Jesus did not. He loved everyone, but how differently! The twelve disciples were his daily companions. But among them there was an inner circle of three or four. And one of those is called 'the disciple whom Jesus loved'. I don't believe Jesus made a 'favourite' of him, but rather that this disciple opened himself more to Jesus' love. Jesus also, as we have seen, loved those he had to criticise. Then he had a special affection for Martha, Mary and Lazarus and liked to stay in their home at Bethany. Many who listened to him and many whom he healed must have felt linked to him by ties of affection. His love went out to still wider circles. He told us to love our enemies and pray for our persecutors, and he did so himself when he prayed for those who were crucifying him: 'Father, forgive.'

This seems impossible, doesn't it? But haven't many of us already discovered that when we try really to pray for someone, we begin to understand them and begin to care for them? And have we not made another discovery? If someone really loves us and we respond, this mutual love overflows on to others and makes us more ready to understand, to care about, to love them. Lots of men and women have discovered also that when we realise—through contemplation and prayer—that we are really loved by God, then his love comes into our hearts and fans out to others. 'We love, because he loved us *first*.' So we need to ask the Holy Spirit to teach us how to prepare to pray.

Immediate Preparation

A friend of mine prepares himself for prayer by walking round his garden, at least on spring mornings and summer evenings. A priest told me that *he* begins his prayer by sitting down with his great dog and either talking to God about his dog or talking to his dog about God. And Archbishop Bloom advised one of his elderly parishioners to sit silent and still and 'knit before the face of God', enjoying the peace of her room. Later she told him in delighted surprise that she had never had such a sense of God's presence. *Chacun selon son goût*. But none of these would work for me!

So may I tell you what I do? And you will discover what is best for yourself. Sometimes frankly I make no preparation at all. I just rush in, as I might to a close friend, blurting out: 'I must tell you, it's so wonderful!' or even: 'Something terrible has happened. I need your help. I need you so much.' Perhaps we should come to God like this more often.

But we can't always. I often have to give myself a push. It's the same in ordinary life. We know we ought to visit a friend, but because we're busy or the weather is bad, or we're lazy that day, we don't feel like going. But fundamentally we are fond of our friend, so we shake ourselves, give ourselves a push, then go—and are usually glad about it afterwards. I often begin my prayer like this, and I will group round three words what I do—quietness, contemplation and the Spirit.

First, I do all I can to have *quietness* around me and

also within me. Needless to say, I don't always succeed. There may be noises outside, or grumblings going on inside me. I try not to be irritated or upset. I may say to God: 'Never mind, let 'em go on; I'm with you, you're with me; that's what matters.' It's like being with a close friend. And I 'shut the door', as Jesus said; and there in my room early in the morning and after the day's work I find myself saying: 'Lord, it is good, really good, to be here.' Those who share a room, I guess, could perhaps discover how to have part of their prayers together and part alone. But their solution must be their own, however unconventional it may be.

I try never to feel in a hurry, even if time has to be short. Haste ruins my praying, as it spoils human fellowship. If I need a little inner 'slowing down', I occasionally read a very few verses of the bible, or some quiet book I know well, like Georges Lefèbvre's *Simplicity*. I never read anything new at this moment, and I must be firmly disciplined to read only just enough to bring me to prayer. Personally I start my actual prayers by saying nothing at all. Silence is normally the doorway as well as the heart of my prayer. I often take a few deep and slow breaths to settle myself down. Some of my friends—and not only those who go in for yoga—do much more about breathing and relaxing before prayer. But this is enough for me to prepare myself to focus on God. Personally I never try deliberately to empty my mind of other thoughts to make a kind of mental vacuum. That just doesn't work for me. For me it's not emptying, but focusing, that matters.

Then next, I try to settle down to prayer in a *contemplative* sort of way. God in his love is always with us and within us. But we need to learn how by simple contemplation to be *aware* of and respond to this love.

And God's love, let us always remember, is not vague and generalised, but individualised love, concentrated totally and separately on you and on me, just as the love—which was in Jesus—was concentrated on Peter in his fears, Thomas in his doubts and the woman of Samaria in her dissimulation by the well. John Dalrymple has well said: 'All the time God is relating to us. All we have to do is to relate back.' I find I need to have ready and prepared different ways of 'relating back' to God. Then I can choose which suits my need on any particular day.

One obvious method is to think of Jesus. This thinking may help to grip our attention. It doesn't itself of course bring Jesus any nearer to us. 'I am with you always' is his promise to us, whatever our feelings may be. I don't use this 'way in' as often as I used to. But an American girl, a friend of mine, far deeper in prayer than I am, tells me she always begins her prayer by looking at the Risen Jesus as he makes a fire to cook breakfast by the lake for his friends, after their long night of fishing—love made man, love meeting men's needs.

A second possible 'way in' is to picture one of the myriad beauties of nature. It is mountains that I love. They 'do' something to me. They give me a sense of the reality and the wonder of God. Glimpses flash back to me from my holidays and my travels—Great Gable seen from Lingmell; that graceful pyramid of the Bietschorn towering above the Rhône valley; the stupendous chain of the Himalayas, seen from a jet; the graceful, snow-rimmed cone of Mt Fuji; or Mt Cook with its twin glittering peaks far, far above us. I am in my own room, silent and overwhelmed again with this beauty, deeply aware of the wonder and of the nearness of God. Other aspects of nature may do the same thing for you—perhaps the English countryside as Constable saw it or the Cornish coastline with its ever-changing sea. Might it help you to have where you pray some pictures like these scenes?

This leads me to a third possible approach—to look in a contemplative spirit at some of the things actually around you at home—a tree seen from your window, a flower in a vase on your table, a holiday snapshot, a picture of a church with deep associations for you; your eyes might rest on a cross or an icon, or you might listen to a little music. In many ways like these your heart and mind may be made aware of the nearness of God.

I could go on making more suggestions—there are perhaps almost as many 'ways in' to prayer as there are people who try to pray. But I must mention a fourth—particularly because this seems at present my own most frequent way. Those mind-pictures don't come to me so much as they used to. However, there is a verse which now so often runs in my mind that it has almost become part of myself, and which we looked at in the last chapter: 'In him we live and move, in him we exist.' I am still, and I say: 'Lord, you are around me and within me, supporting and sustaining me like the air I breathe —you, who are love itself, that love I see in Jesus.' Somehow I am held by this love. I don't always feel it, any more than I usually feel the air I am breathing, but it is there, it is real. This divine love is frequently—as a man of God paradoxically once said—'too deep to be felt'.

We may find that different ways of approaching prayer help us at different stages of our lives. We should never be too nostalgic. We mustn't say: 'It used to feel so real, but now I hardly feel anything.' Feelings are important, but by themselves they are unreliable tests. Human love also sometimes grows less intense, without becoming any less genuine or any less deep. In fact it may become almost imperceptibly even deeper and more unifying. In prayer as in love we can never forecast. Let us be ready for whatever comes. It is wiser to be flexible, to have several ways of quietly holding on in our prayer, as I have said, according to changing days and seasons. But don't let us flit about from one approach to another. If we have discovered a well-tried way—as long as it doesn't become mere routine—let us keep to it. It has become the loved greeting of One who is more than a friend.

And finally—for me it is essential—I ask for the help of the *Spirit* of God. More and more I am finding as I wait like this at the threshold of prayer—but I am not quite sure whether it is the threshold—that I say in words or in silence something like this:

> I can't pray. I try to be still, to be ready. But that's all.
> If I'm really to pray, Lord, you must help me.
> May your Spirit show me the way to pray that is best for me.
> May I really bring to you, *Abba*, my Father, those dear to me.

And as we come to prayer we must try always to be expectant. 'Seek, and you will find.' If we expect nothing, nothing much usually happens. We may feel nothing, but something happens deeper than we know. Another experience of ours helps us to understand this. It happens after we have been very ill. We have passed the critical point of our illness, and our energy is deep down beginning to return. But we feel nothing of it.

For a long time we ask: 'Shall I ever feel strong again?' Then one day at last we can say: 'Yes, without my noticing it, my strength has been returning and now I *know* it.' So in the life of prayer let us *expect* the light and love of the Spirit, and eventually we shall know it. If we give good gifts to our children, then 'how much more', Jesus says, 'will the heavenly Father give the Holy Spirit to those who ask him?' The Spirit is the giver of true prayer, through whom alone we can really and confidently say 'Abba, Father'.

And now I can almost hear someone asking: 'When are you going to get to telling us about praying itself? You are spending all this time in preparing for prayer. If we take your advice, all our time will be taken up with preparing to pray and we shan't get down to praying at all.' 'But,' I would reply, 'would that matter very much?'

God doesn't need our words; he reads our hearts. Archbishop Michael Ramsey said that praying for others is coming to God with those we care for in our hearts. Let us try to do our best to come to him; and he'll take care of the rest.

Perhaps we could reflect on this for a moment. If you and I normally prepared more deeply for our prayer, don't you think we should pray better for others? So perhaps it is more true than we used to think that 'the preparation for prayer may surpass in spiritual value prayer itself'.

5

JOYS AND
RESPONSIBILITIES
SHARED

*The nature of love is such that it shares every-
thing.*

Cloud of Unknowing

ALONE in my room or on the hills, when I step back
from life, I realise that basically there are two ways of
living. Nearly all of us, I suppose, fall somewhere between the two. The first is the determination to 'get
things done'; it may lead to great achievements, but
often with unhappy side-effects. The other is the way
of partnership; you realise you are appreciated, understood and perhaps loved. You respond, you begin to
share. Out of this partnership, something overflows
into the jobs of life; they don't become less; but they
are enriched with considerateness, resilience, joy,
douceur, a growing love. The apostle Paul had 'drive';
but we see it maturing, both through his understanding of partnership—'thankful for your partnership in
the gospel', he wrote to his friends—and through his
increasing experience of the mercy and love of God
through Jesus Christ.

So it is also in the unfolding life of contemplation
and prayer. We think of prayer—as I used to do as a

boy—as a way of getting things done. But more and more we come to see prayer as a growing partnership with God—things are 'done' through prayer, but done through love divine and human. 'If I have all faith, so as to remove mountains, but have not love, I am nothing.'

I have said already that I myself need two times of prayer each day. For me morning prayer is 'receiving-prayer', rather contemplative—helping me to dwell in the Lord, to receive his love and to respond. My evening prayer is 'giving-prayer', sharing with the Lord the joys and responsibilities of daily life.

Of course each one of us must discover our own way. 'Pray as you can', Dom John Chapman repeatedly said, 'Don't pray as you can't.'

In this chapter I would like to tell you what I try to do in the evening. It doesn't always come off like this. I hope you won't mind, but I think I'd better speak personally. Perhaps personal details may help you more than vague generalisations. Sometimes happiness or trouble makes me just 'burst' into prayer. Always I like to be spontaneous; but I have a hidden, *underlying* pattern, as I will soon explain. Without some sort of basic pattern—and you can design one of your own—our relationship with God can become unrealistic and unbalanced, as friendships can too. Even so, my prayers vary very much from day to day. I have in the preceding chapter told you about my 'way in'.

Adoration

As soon as I have settled down, I usually pause and wonder at what is happening now. God is here welcoming me, as the father in the parable welcomed the son. I may not feel it, but I'm sure of it. And I can—through the Spirit—respond, '*Abba*, my own Father'. But this intimacy is enfolded within wonder. For God is infinitely beyond us, in 'deep but dazzling darkness'. For Jesus too, God was the Lord, the creator of heaven and earth, enthroned, high and lifted up; yet Jesus said his *Abba*. And our knowledge of the immensity of the universe makes us realise even more the enormous gap between God and us. It is further widened by the contrast between the loving holiness of God and our own numberless failings and vacillations. And to cross that gap it required all the divine love, seen in the coming, living, dying and rising of Christ—in order to bring us our forgiveness, unite us to God and set us free for his service of love. I am, again and again, amazed at all this. Sometimes I am silent in wonder; sometimes words of praise and adoration come spontaneously to my lips. And when I am alone, I don't just think these words, I say them quietly. For me, saying words expresses love and also deepens it.

> O Love, how deep, how broad, how high,
> How passing thought and fantasy.

Sometimes a good deal of my evening prayer-time is passed like this. I can't quite find a word for this experience. Adoration is as good as any.

Let us notice in passing that adoration is not a servile cringing before God; nor does God desire our adoration as flattering praise. He desires our adoration because he loves us; and incidentally because adoration turns us away from those petty egoisms and self-preoccupations which spoil our life and service of others. If in adoration we forget 'self', we may gradually come to forget 'self' in our serving others. 'Adoration disinfects our service of others from egoism.' Baron Friedrich von Hügel used to call adoration the heart of religion; and you didn't really know von Hügel with all his many gifts, it was said, unless you had seen his massive head bowed before God in adoration.

Repentance

When we come to God in adoration, we sense our own unworthiness. The brighter the sunlight, the darker the shadow, inevitably. At the moment when Isaiah perceived the glory of God he felt within himself his own faults and the faults of his nation. So each evening I face my faults, particularly those of the past day—my lack of understanding towards someone who called to see me, my laziness in taking twice as long as I ought over some work, or my share in a weak-kneed decision of the church I belong to. These things come to me without any excessive introspection. God knows these faults already. It is for my own good that he wishes me to own up to them. I must be realistic. God does not condone, he forgives.

How much it sometimes costs a friend to forgive us! How much our forgiveness costs the divine love—we have just reflected on it—the love disclosed in Jesus and his unceasing service with its culmination on the cross. As in my room I confess, I remember this, I remain silent. Then I receive into my heart this forgiveness from God and his strength. I slowly make the sign of the cross as a sign of my accepting this mercy. Outward signs are as valuable in prayer as in love. And I must try the next day to attack these faults in the strength God has given me. I must also try to pardon others' faults. 'Forgive us our trespasses, as we forgive those who trespass against us.' So repentance and forgiveness are the second element in my evening prayer and lead on naturally to thanksgiving.

Thankfulness

I don't count my blessings; I reflect on them in my heart. Personally I have to begin with what is real to me, what touches me, or else my gratitude easily becomes just words. I thank God for others, for the joy I see in their eyes, for the love and courage in their lives. But when I have begun there, then my thankfulness spreads out—how it does, I will mention later in this chapter. And often I am again 'lost in wonder, love and praise'.

I sometimes manage to thank God—though not always at once—for unpleasant experiences, 'blessings incognito'. I myself don't believe that God directly sends them to us. But these experiences can sometimes open our eyes to covered-up facts about ourselves; and, even more important, they can widen our sympathies for others, who have similar misfortunes, and so make us more able to understand and love them. When we have been in trouble, how often we have turned confidently to a friend who has been through trouble, and said to ourselves: 'I know *he* will understand.' Our disappointments and frustrations can, through God's help, transform us into men and women of deeper love. The more we can thank God, the better. Thankfulness strengthens our love for God, deepens our love of our friends, and brings us happiness. And happiness—let us always remember—although not the most important thing in life, is important, because happiness refreshes our mind and heart, and silences that egoistical, complaining monologue which can so easily fill up our time. If we think it over, we see that we live either thankfully or resentfully. C. S. Lewis used to say: 'Praise is an audible sign of health'; and he added that 'the most balanced and capacious minds praise most, while cranks, misfits and malcontents praise least'. Paul in his life full of hazards wrote: 'Give thanks whatever happens,' meaning that we should give thanks not *for* all circumstances but *in* all circumstances. 'It is our duty and our joy,' we sing again and again in our eucharist, 'at all times and in all places to give you thanks and praise, holy Father, heavenly King.' My daily thanksgiving in my room draws me into this joyful, worldwide orchestra of praise.

Intercession

And then in gratitude my thoughts turn naturally to my friends. God has drawn us near to him and in his love he draws us together. Because we love, we pray. However far apart, we know that we are one *in* him, whose love and presence interpenetrates all. Through our desires and prayers, as much as by our actions and letters, God can convey his strength and love to them. We may perhaps have spoken about our friends in gratitude earlier in our prayers; and why not speak about them to God again? Prayer is not going through a list of names, like a shopping list or a school register: it is openly and spontaneously 'sharing' with God our joy in others, our hopes for them, our fears and difficulties.

And we know we ourselves deeply need the prayers of our friends. We ask for their prayers, as Paul did so often in his letters, as Jesus asked of the disciples in the garden of Gethsemane. We all stand in need of this ceaseless flow of prayer and love:

> For so the whole round earth is every way
> Bound by gold chains about the feet of God.

But there are in various parts of the world so many others we feel we ought to pray for. Their names can easily become a mere catalogue and prayer a mumbo-jumbo. I shall never forget what a nun once said to me about this problem. In her community throughout the day and night they take turns to pray for an hour for people whose names have been sent to them. 'How, Sister, can this be real prayer?' I asked her. 'How can you keep it from becoming mere routine?' She answered: 'When I go to chapel for my hour of intercession, I first settle down and remember God and his love, going out ceaselessly to each one of his creatures. Then I look at the long list in front of me. I can always recognise a few people I know or whose needs I can understand. Then I throw myself with all my love into praying for them. And, as I do this, I find my love grows enough to overflow into the other intercessions. In prayer as in life, love expressed is love that grows.'

That is why I usually begin my own intercessions with those I care for—you of course may have a different starting point—and for those for whom I have some personal responsibility. As I try to do this, I find love and the desire to pray grows. Prayer spreads like ripples on a pond, once you have thrown in a great stone.

So my prayer ripples out—and always in different ways—to people I have spoken to or written to that day, to some I know who have to carry heavy responsibilities at home or on the other side of the world. This wider intercession I find—perhaps you do too—needs a certain amount of planning, but not too much. I will return to this question towards the end of this chapter.

63

I find it hard to explain exactly how this praying for others 'works'. But I am sure that it does. This is the conviction of millions of men and women, and some of them very acute, intelligent people. Prayer, we believe, is a privilege God has given us, *the privilege of collaborating with him* in gradually bringing about the transformation of the world. God could presumably do without our efforts and our prayers, but he doesn't. For example, in healing someone who is ill, God normally waits for the doctor and nurse and patient to work together with him. And if God waits for our collaboration in action, may he not wait for our collaboration in prayer? He intends in this way, I think, to help us to understand, to support, to love one another. Love is his kingdom and the road to it.

The healing of the paralysed man, brought on a stretcher to Jesus by his friends, could be a picture of our intercession. Jesus had the desire and the power to help the man. Yet humanly speaking it looks as if the man would not have been helped unless his friends had brought him to Jesus. And for this effort those friends had to have both love enough to give up the time to bring the man, and also confidence in Jesus that he would help. Our confidence in God grows deeper, I believe, through contemplation. So the more we wish to intercede, the more we should think about contemplation.

But what often discourages us from intercession is our past experience of 'unanswered prayer'. We pray and pray for someone we love, and nothing happens. We feel hurt and shaken. I know this experience myself. We cannot put down our unanswered prayers simply to our lack of faith. For Jesus, although he never lacked faith, experienced unanswered prayer. He prayed that Peter's faith should not fail, and he saw it fail that night.

God receives all our prayers—that is the basis of all that Jesus teaches. Then we must leave it to God's love and wisdom how these prayers are answered. 'Thy will be done.' But, if God's will for the person prayed for is going to be done in any case, you may ask: 'Why go on praying?' Whatever praying we do, it appears, is not going to make much difference.

God respects us, as responsible men and women, as —we may dare to say—his collaborators. God may well, as I said a few minutes ago, do something with our collaboration—collaboration both in prayer and in action—which he would not will to do *without* us. Nor must we give up our praying for others or for ourselves too soon, even if nothing seems to happen. The waiting may sometimes for various reasons be for the ultimate good of others and of ourselves. Let me point out one of these reasons. In our pride we may believe that we can get all sorts of things done quickly by our practical efficiency or by the earnestness of our own prayers. This delay may shake this false belief and bring home to us our real, practical dependence on God. For there may be many things, good in themselves, which God could not wisely nor safely give us through prayer, while we are still running this feverish temperature of pride and self-sufficiency. Archbishop William Temple once spoke about this to a group of students; he said that beef-steak is good, but you don't give it to a man in a high fever; you bring his temperature down first, and only then will he enjoy the steak and will it do him any good. *Our* temperature must be brought down. Few things are more unrealistic, more distressing to our friends, more damaging in the world, or more insulating from God than an exaggerated trust in our own competence in action or in prayer. St Augustine knew this and perhaps he had it in mind when he wrote about our persevering in prayer: 'God does not ask us to tell him our needs that he may learn about them, but in order that we may be *capable of receiving* what he is preparing to give.'

So we need to persist in prayer; and prayer is sometimes far from easy. We see this vividly in Jesus' prayer in the garden of Gethsemane. There Jesus gave himself to God that he might be given for men. And when we really pray for a person or for some cause, we are *in the same breath* offering ourselves in love to be used by God through whatever opportunity may be opened up. And if what we hoped for does not open up, then God takes our love and our prayers, I am convinced, and uses them in ways beyond our reckoning both for those we pray for—and also for those who live on our doorstep. So through our praying for others perhaps far away, God also builds up round about us families and groups of friends, whose love, influence, *rayonnement* in the world may surpass all our expectations.

Although, as I have said, I find it hard to explain how prayer 'works', I would like to probe a little further. What I am going to say is no more than a reasonable speculation. But it has incidentally helped me and some of my friends to integrate praying with living.

If sincerely we pray for others, we really give ourselves to God—as I said a moment ago—for him to use as part of his answering of our prayers. So in genuine intercession we desire to give God not only our words, but our minds, our hearts, and the depths of our personality. It is at these hidden depths—there is evidence enough, I think, for this—that we can touch one another. We are aware of this with our friends. As we walk together through the woods, we may say little, but we are close to each other at this deep level. And this contact can be extended far beyond our friends. John Donne wrote:

No man is an island, entire of itself;
Every man is a piece of a continent, a part of the
main.

We look like the isolated islands of the Caribbean. In fact they are beneath the ocean connected by means of the seabed. We too are connected, but unfortunately we do not communicate well with one another. Yet I believe God intends this natural connection to become the circuit of his love—the love all men need.

Our misfortune is that instead of being conductors of God's love, we are insulators because of our self-sufficiency and egoism. But we can be changed if progressively we open ourselves to the Spirit of God. We need—if I may use an inadequate analogy from physics —to be transformed from being insulating black mica to become pure conducting copper wire. If we intercede sincerely and frequently, I am convinced the Spirit of God transmutes us. We then both receive God's love into our hearts and also transmit it to others. Intercession becomes, as George Stewart called it, 'our communion with God *for others*'. In fact if through intercession God's love flows freely through us, it will also permeate the way we speak to one another, the way we write letters, the way we carry out responsibilities in the world and progressively it will alter our whole lifestyle. So the secular activities of our lives will constitute, as Dr Oliver Quick used to say, 'the very substance and matter of what we offer in prayer'. These reflections are only a beginning; I have much to explore in the mystery of intercession.

Prayer for Oneself

Some people think it's selfish to pray for yourself. I don't agree. Jesus told us to love others not instead of ourselves but *as* ourselves. If we don't pray adequately about our own spiritual, as well as our physical and intellectual health, we're not likely to be able to take true care of others.

First, I must pray honestly. It's so easy to pretend. In my prayers I must come out with my hopes and fears, my joy and my 'fed-upness'. Don Camillo's violent words, said before the altar, about the communist mayor, were not blasphemous, but authentic. What is inside our hearts let us put in God's hands for him to deal with.

Next, I know I must share with God my ordinary material life. Jesus told his disciples to ask for bread. I must speak to him about all the things I have to do. I must realise that my work is not mine, that I work in his service in fellowship with him. Charles de Foucauld said: 'There must be nothing indirect in our prayers.' We must pray straightforwardly, asking for what we want, though adding: 'Not as I will, but as you will.' Need and asking are so essential to our human nature that any minimising, let alone suppressing them, would be a crippling of our personality.

Then, I must see my praying—far from being another burden on top of all my other work—as quietly unifying my life, seeing it all within God's over-arching purpose of love. In this prayer I stand back for a moment and *see*. I realise afresh that I am loved by God and that basically I want to respond and to know how to respond in my own particular situation. I need to ask as Solomon did—so it is in the original Hebrew—for 'a listening heart'.

Finally, I must, as we have seen, go on and on asking. Paul repeatedly asked that some complaint he had—'a thorn in the flesh'—might be taken away, but it was not. He had to learn to live with it. He found he could. And in his weakness he discovered—at a depth which he might otherwise never have known—God's power in his own life. 'When I am weak,' he wrote, 'then am I strong.' We like Paul must be prepared in the end for 'No'—the 'No' of love. This bringing of my own needs to God is the fifth section of my prayer, and leads round again to love and confidence.

Trust in God

Praying about and feeling the vast problems of our world, I may be disorientated by them. And if we are disorientated, we can't effectively and lovingly serve others. So I return to trust in God. But trust must not be unrealistic. Life is fairly tough for most of us. God's promise to us, Mother Julian reminds us, is not 'Thou shalt not be tempested' but 'Thou shalt not be overcome'. So I always end my prayers with words of firm trust in God, like those of Isaiah, prophet and politician, in dark and anxious days:

> Thou dost keep in peace men of constant mind, in peace because they trust in thee.
> Trust in the Lord for ever, for the Lord himself is an everlasting rock.

And trust, like love, grows through being repeatedly expressed; and leads to joy. Prayer must always be open-eyed; yet, like the conversation of those who love each other, fundamentally joyful. It was the Latin-American poet, Ernesto Cardenal, in his struggle for justice, who wrote: 'Joy can be a perfect prayer, because it is an act of confidence in God. And joy can sometimes be heroic.'

This account of my evening prayer must sound longer and more complicated than it actually is. This scheme—the successive sections—is actually telescopic. It is equally suitable for ten minutes' prayer or for an hour's.

I don't care much for formulas of prayer. But you may have noticed that the initial letters of these six sections of my prayer—adoration, repentance, thanksgiving, intercession, self (prayers for myself) and trust—form a key-word, *artist*. I'm all for keeping prayers spontaneous. But guidelines for normal occasions have their uses. This particular sequence reminds us that praying is not primarily asking, but loving, growing into our true partnership with God and with others.

Distractions

I said at the very beginning of this book that I would try to keep it practical. So I would like to wind up this chapter by looking at two practical matters—dealing with distractions and being systematic. I simply must say something about distractions in prayer. Everyone is bothered by them. A wandering thought can be a jab of conscience; if so, I pray about it briefly and then return to my sequence of prayer. Occasionally a distraction is something important, not to be forgotten. So I always keep beside me where I pray—and also by my bed at night time—a small writing pad; I jot down these important things briefly at once, then I can safely forget them and pick them up afterwards.

But some of our wandering thoughts are unimportant; and others we can do nothing about at the time. If a young man at his evening prayers suddenly remembers that he has forgotten to put through an important phone call for his firm—and that'll mean a row—it is useless for him to worry about it. The only thing is to try to turn away from it to God as quickly as he can. Nor must we be annoyed at wandering thoughts, as annoyance may be a sign of our pride. We are humiliated that we are not 'as concentrated at prayer' as we thought we were! St Francis de Sales used to say that, if in our time of prayer our thoughts wander a hundred times, we must not worry; because if we can come back to God each time unruffled, these thoughts have done no harm and we have turned back to God and have so given him a hundred signs of our love for him; probably that time of prayer was better than those rarer occasions when prayer seems to go smoothly.

There are times when we are terribly distracted in prayer. We are in pain, or are worried about someone we love, or are impatiently waiting for a vital letter. At these times I have found it a help to open a book of prayers or psalms or hymns, and to pray by reading some of them slowly. God understands. Prayer is not feeling pleased with ourselves, but trying in spite of obstacles to respond to God's love.

But one of the more effective ways of dealing with distractions—though it sounds so prosaic—is simply to begin your prayer well, really settle down for prayer. If we don't begin well, we're not likely to go on well.

Being Systematic

When I was speaking both about thanksgiving and also about intercession, I said it was vital that our prayers should spread out from our personal, deeply-felt concerns to those of the wider world.

This came home to me when I was working with a Sister among displaced children. We wanted them in their uprooted life to pray and really to trust God. So we helped them to make their own books of prayer with something special to pray for and something special to thank God for each day. As soon as we finished that project, the Sister to my great surprise put into my hands a large looseleaf notebook on the same lines—but with magnificent lettering and old masters and other pictures pasted in to illustrate the themes. In my gratitude I used it for years, slipping my personal lists of thanksgivings and intercessions into the appropriate days and revising them from time to time.

As a possible basis for you to adopt, reject or modify, perhaps I might share it with you. I pray much more spontaneously than you might guess from this outline. The themes are all filled out with local colour and names. I'm never dominated by my scheme. Sometimes I scrap it all and just pour out to God what is in my heart. It is our living relationship with him that matters. But here is my basic skeleton scheme. It gets clothed with the warm living flesh of daily prayer.

Thanksgivings

    Sunday joy of our Lord's resurrection;

    Monday   wonder of creation and God's care for all;

    Tuesday   love of God seen all through the life of Jesus;

    Wednesday   Holy Spirit who renews our love and prayer;

    Thursday   love of God in the eucharist and scriptures;

Friday   love of God, disclosed in Jesus' passion;
Saturday   people of God, spanning space and time.

Intercessions
Sunday   universal Church, clergy and people I have visited;
Monday   racial and social relationships, right use of resources;
Tuesday   peace, mission and world-aid;
Wednesday   education, communications, schools and colleges I know;
Thursday   friends, the lonely, prisoners, the unjustly treated;
Friday   the suffering, the aged, doctors and nurses, social services;
Saturday   unity of mankind, the departed and communion of saints.

The notebook the Sister gave me collapsed in the end through hard, daily loving use. I have replaced it with others, smaller ones, easier to handle in travelling. Alan Ecclestone in his *Yes to God*, a prize-winning book rich in his own love of literature and in his deep social concern, recommends the very same thing. He tells us to put into a looseleaf notebook or into an interleaved printed book of worship some great prayers, which we have found for ourselves, with poems, pictures, fragments of letters and our own personal lists, reflections and questions we must face; he calls it 'the work-book of our life'.

Would you consider whether it might deepen your prayers if you had some pattern for them—my *artist* sequence or something quite different? And perhaps some 'work-book' of your own life *gradually* compiled on your own plan—and why not with pictures and colours?—might help you on those days when your enthusiasm of love ebbs. It does ebb a bit. If we are to grow in love, we need every bit of help we can get; at least I do.

6

REFLECTIVE READING

We nourish our faith, we stimulate our hope, we establish our confidence by these holy utterances.

TERTULLIAN

You may remember the children's story of the rabbit and the toy horse, lying side by side near the fender before anyone came in to tidy up the playroom.

'What is *real*?' asked the rabbit.

'Real isn't how you are made,' said the toy horse, 'it's a thing that happens to you. When a child loves you for a long, long time, not just to play with, but really loves you, then you become real.'

'Does it happen all at once,' he asked, 'or bit by bit?'

'It doesn't happen all at once,' said the horse. 'You become. But it takes a *long* time.'

We all want to become real through receiving love and responding with love. We long to be awakened to what we are, to become our real selves. This is what contemplation is all about.

On the human level we all need in many different forms to receive and to give love if we are to grow to maturity. In human friendship and affection the receiving and the giving are often fused. At times we may be more aware of one than the other. Yet sometimes we are strangely reluctant to admit our need to receive. It is,

I think, due sometimes to our egoistical self-sufficiency. We mean to get things done by ourselves. We are determined unaided to be masters of our fate and captains of our souls. It may take us a long time to learn the art of receiving appreciatively, genuinely and graciously. But when we do, we realise that this wonderful capacity for receiving was there all the time, fallow. But what a joy to see it coming to life!

It is the same in the life of faith and prayer. God can give, when we have learned how to receive. And St Bernard says: 'In giving himself to me God has *made me myself.*' We need receiving-prayer and giving-prayer. These also tend to fuse. But, as we saw in the last chapter, my evening prayers are chiefly giving-prayer—my adoration, repentance, thankfulness, intercession, petition for myself—given to God in love and trust. It is my morning prayers that are chiefly for receiving.

You may have already embarked—or re-embarked—on giving-prayer. So far so good. But from receiving-prayer it is easy to hold back. We are often slower to acknowledge our need for it and unsure about our capacity for religious contemplation. Yet we saw at the opening of this book how widespread are beginnings of natural contemplation. However unused and dormant it has been, the capacity to 'contemplate', like the capacity to receive human love, can with help and encouragement be discovered and developed.

Receiving-prayer leading towards contemplative praying is valuable to us all. First, a quiet contemplative looking towards God may often be our best way to enter into all our other kinds of prayer—giving-prayer, informal prayer together and worship. But, secondly, it is largely through contemplative prayer

76

that we discover how to be *open* to God, how to receive his love and so—through his Spirit—how to respond to it. Our capacity will grow and so will our need. This will be a joy. 'How blest are those who know their need of God.' As in human love, we may have to experience some growing-pains; but those pains are well worth bearing. Then, thirdly, as the interaction of love begins to happen at depth, we shall find God uses our prayer and our work probably far more than we should expect to bring his kingdom into the world. So contemplative prayer is not only for our own enrichment, but for the transformation of the world.

What should we Read?

So perhaps you would like to take a step with me in the direction of contemplative praying. We would like our capacity for receptive prayer aroused and developed. One important method for this is leisurely reading of a particular kind of book—the books and letters of those who have made this journey before us. I am not now writing about specialised academic reading of the bible or of technical books on the life of prayer, important as that must be for some people—those, for example, who are responsible for guiding others. I am thinking now of ordinary men and women who want encouragement to pray and live contemplatively.

For us, five or ten minutes with the writings and memoirs of earlier explorers can be very valuable when we sit for a rest—or perhaps for our bedtime reading. These books, or parts of them, we can and should read over and over again. We are reading now not to gain new information but to awaken our desire for prayer, especially for a simple beginning of contemplative praying; and we mustn't go reading on and on. Read a little, ponder much. These are minutes we shall come to look forward to—a time to grow in love.

We might choose first from among the Christian classics which have been loved all down the ages: for instance, we could read parts of the *Confessions* of St Augustine, St Francis de Sales' *Introduction to the Devout Life*, Bunyan's *Pilgrim's Progress* or that great prototype, Thomas à Kempis' *The Imitation of Christ*. Though this last book, which I treasure, I find, as I have said, too negative in places. A sophisticated non-churchgoing woman used to keep it at her bedside and read a few verses every night with a wry kind of admiration, 'as a reminder', she said, 'of all I could never be'. Then there are the great prayerful books of our own day, like William Temple's *Readings in St John's Gospel* and Bonhoeffer's *Life Together*. We need to be selective, and find what suits us and the purpose of these quiet moments, being content with short passages which deepen our desire to advance in receptive prayer.

People ask me whether they should use at these times books of prayer of other faiths. I am not sure that I know enough to answer that question. I myself have found helpful some beautiful Moslem prayers which Kenneth Cragg has selected and published in his book, *Alive to God*. Many people could well dip into a small book, simply entitled *Prayer*, by a French monk who took the name Abhishiktananda. He uses wisely elements of Hindu spirituality to deepen our Christian prayer. In general I think we should try to appreciate the sincere faiths of other people, but to do so outside our times of prayerful reading. Yet Christian friends of mine tell me they have gained much from eastern spirituality. But I myself think it unwise in so profound and sensitive an area of our lives to try to make any artificially synthetic faith.

What about the Bible?

We can hardly respond to Someone we don't know; and we can't become our 'real selves', unless we go in search of Reality. I myself am now convinced that God the supreme Reality has disclosed himself to us in an unparalleled way in Jesus. We are not likely to come to know Jesus without the bible. So our next step should be in my opinion to equip ourselves for an intelligent and prayerful use of the bible.

I must be honest and say how much the bible means to me personally for my prayers; but I can understand how to some people, even to some Christians, it seems very remote. Again I am concerned here with the bible not as a book for academic study, although I have spent years of my life lecturing on it, but as *a book for prayer*; though naturally there is no sharp boundary between these two uses.

It is practically impossible to write a few lines about the historical background of the bible. But without some background it is not easy to use the bible for our prayers. First, we need to keep on reminding ourselves that the bible is not what it looks like, a book, but a whole library. It spoils the bible to read its allegories as history, its poetry as prose, its legal codes as life in its richness. Secondly, perhaps the most fascinating thing about this 'library', written over a period as long as that from the Norman conquest of England until today, can be the most easily lost. I mean man's gradual, step-by-step discovery of God and his love for us—or rather, God's step-by-step disclosure of himself and of his love for us. This is why we are not worried at some crudity in parts of the bible which come from early times. Nor are we disturbed by the fact that the progress has not been a steady one, for only too often man has closed his eyes to God's leading. So man has often found himself learning more from his tragedies than from his blessings. Thirdly, for prayerful reading the gospels stand on a level entirely by themselves. And for our present purpose, the Old Testament is of value chiefly as the background of Jesus; and the rest of the New Testament as showing the impact of Jesus on his first followers and on the early Church.

You might study, outside your times of prayerful reading, one background book on the bible; William Neil's *Rediscovery of the Bible*, or his *Bible Story* could be enough. And you will have to decide for yourself what translation you are going to use. I would advise a modern translation *with notes*—the *Annotated Revised Standard Version*, the *Jerusalem Bible*, or A. E. Harvey's *Companion to the New Testament* (*New English Bible*). One of these is worth buying—or asking for as a birthday present—because their notes are all the commentary most of us need, at least for prayerful reading of the bible.

If you are just starting or starting again to read the bible in this way, I would recommend Stephen Neill's *One Increasing Purpose*, which gives you a whole panorama of the bible story in selected passages for two months. The Bible Reading Fellowship (2 Elizabeth Street, London SW1W 9RQ) publish it and also several graded series of daily bible notes. The Scripture Union (5 Wigmore Street, London W1) issue similar series, rather more conservative in outlook. Daily notes are useful in helping us to train ourselves into reading the bible regularly.

The Gospels

After a time—if you are an independently-minded reader like myself—you may wish to choose your own line. I think we shall find a need to go through the gospels again and again. You might like, outside your time of prayer, to read in a new translation one gospel straight through and catch its special flavour. I enjoy doing this. Mark writes of Jesus with a sense of immediacy in a vivid, almost breathless style. Matthew shows us our ever-present divine Lord with his roots in history. Luke pictures the universal Jesus, whom we shall understand better as we move into the future. John's gospel is the simplest, the most profound, the most contemplative.

Then we could go through one gospel a paragraph at a time, reading, reflecting, praying, like handling and admiring the separate beads in a necklace. Should any passage seem unhelpful, we could pass it over, at least for the time being. We might start with four readings in the first chapter of Mark. In the first thirteen verses, we see that Jesus doesn't come as a bolt from the blue; and as then, so now we prepare to meet him. Then at our next reading in verses 14–20, we notice Jesus has partners in his work. On the next occasion in verses 21–34 we reflect on a typical day for Jesus. Finally, as we finish this chapter, we are struck by how vital prayer is for him, even in all this pressure of work.

We shouldn't say about passages from the gospels: 'I have read them before, I know them', because we come to our prayerful reading, not to be better informed, but to begin to know Jesus, and God, whom he discloses, more personally and more intimately. When we have read a letter from a close friend, we often put it into our wallet or handbag, because we know we shall want to read it again. Each reading of the letter brings our friend to us, and so do the gospels. The gospels are our 'written meetings' with the Lord.

And what an effect the gospels can have on us! One student in search of a spiritual guide made two trips to India. On the second he came across a Christian ashram and decided, for a six-month trial period, to take Jesus as if he were an Indian guru. The young man, brought up in an agnostic home, was still vague about God and couldn't accept the miracles in the gospels. He decided to read the gospels seriously, and to follow as literally as he could the teaching of Jesus and see what happened. In six months he knew he was a Christian and had begun to receive the Lord in holy communion. It happened like falling in love, he says; but, like that experience, pointed to something far deeper always to come. God answered his prayers; but prayer is essentially loving, he now knows, not asking. He has left his mountain of Transfiguration for the dusty plain, but its effect remains; at least he finds himself less irritable and more outgoing than he used to be.

The Old Testament

We should, I think, turn sometimes to the more unfamiliar Old Testament for *our prayerful, reflective reading*. Without it we shall not really understand Jesus. He was brought up on it. Jesus needed Mary to give him birth. He needed his disciples and friends to draw out his true humanity by their questions and affection. And he needed the Old Testament scriptures. True, he knew inwardly, as we have seen, his unparalleled relationship with God. He had this relationship *within* himself. But to think about it and about his life-task, and to speak about them to his followers, he needed those words and images, which he took from the Old Testament. He took them, reshaped them, re-arranged them in an inspired way. But to understand what Jesus was saying and doing, we have to see how these words and images occur in the Hebrew writings. Yet to use this rich medley of Hebrew scriptures for our reflective reading, we certainly need a guide. What-ever I could say here would be too brief to be useful. Perhaps, if you are really a beginner, I might ask you to begin the Old Testament by reading slowly a few selected Psalms, for they were Jesus' worship-book. I love some of the Psalms; let me mention half-a-dozen— 23, 46, 67, 103, 121, 148. What do you make of them? I wish I knew which Psalms you discover for yourselves in the ups and downs of life as real prayers of love and confidence.

The Letters of the New Testament

Although many of us turn most frequently to the gospels for our prayerful reading, we should sometimes go to the epistles. Remember again why we are doing this—primarily to deepen our love for God. I myself still prefer to read them in J. B. Phillips' paperback, *Letters to Young Churches*. This edition has been out some years; in fact I think it opened the way for the flood of modern translations. It puts these letters briefly into their context. And you won't forget, will you, that the Acts of the Apostles is the background book for these letters of Paul?

If I were going to start on the epistles, I should choose the one to the Philippians. Let me tell you in some detail how I would set about. It's a good letter to start with, fairly easy to understand and the most affectionate of Paul's letters, except his charming note to Philemon. I should begin by reminding myself that Paul was in prison, with plenty of worries on his mind. His friends in Philippi—many of them close friends—had their difficulties too. They had suffered persecution; they had cliques in their church; two women were having a real row; visiting preachers were bothering them with a strange, half-Jewish, half-Christian message. Paul doesn't mince his words about those visitors. We could sit down and read this letter right through in a quarter of an hour. We could look at Paul's first eventful contact with these friends at Philippi in chapter 16 of the Acts.

We notice in the first chapter of the letter Paul's prayer and deep concern for his friends; the second chapter is about their affairs, particularly their dissensions, a bit under the surface; in the third Paul fairly 'lays in' to these strange teachers; and the fourth chapter is a kind of farewell message. (Of course, Paul did not write letters in chapters and verses, any more than you and I do; these are artificialities inserted centuries later.) We could next divide the letter up into about a dozen sections; the modern translations or J. B. Phillips show where the natural divisions come.

I should use these short sections one after another for my prayerful reading on successive days—perhaps ten minutes or more a day. The apostle's prayer in the opening twelve verses would be enough for me for the first day. I should set about it roughly in this way. I should begin by being still, as I mentioned in chapter 4. Then because Christians believe that in various ways the bible writers were helped and inspired by the Holy Spirit, I should pray briefly in this sort of way:

Paul was helped by you, Spirit of God,
   in his daily living, in his writing and in his pray-
      ing;
Help me now as I try to read, to pray,
   to receive your love and share it with others.

Next I should read the passage slowly without looking
at any notes, and try to understand it for myself. Afterwards I might look at any notes given in my modern
version. I remind myself again I am not here primarily
to study, but to pray. I should reflect leisurely for myself and what I should look for chiefly would be anything disclosed about God or about prayer which might
help me.

In these particular dozen verses Paul puts thanking
before interceding. We all know how even in our times
of praying, we can feel superior and patronising: 'Let
us pray for poor old So-and-so,' we say, 'he's got himself
into trouble again.' It would be better to put our thanking before our asking, as Paul does here; and he even
does this when he begins to write to Christians in
Corinth—and they were a terrible lot!

And Paul, we notice in these verses, is praying with
joy, with confidence and with love, human love inter-
penetrated with divine love; for he says: 'I have you in
my heart' and then adds: 'I long for you all in the
heart of Christ Jesus.' And he prays that their love may
be open-eyed.

Towards the end of my time of reflection I should
see if this passage suggested anything useful for me to
do at once. And I should always finish my prayer,
again, with a few words of gratitude and confidence in
God.

I am not putting in this book these examples of slow

meditative prayers as a substitute for your own reflecting and praying. Of course if you would like to use them in your times of prayer, do; but if so, use them very slowly with frequent pauses; or, better still, expand them in your own way. It is seldom much good reading other people's prayers. We need something which is our own. This does not mean that we cannot pray someone else's prayer at all. Indeed he may put into words what we are trying to say. In fact what we need to do is to put *ourselves* into the prayer. You can't sing a love-song, unless you are in love. We can't really pray, unless at least we *want* to love God. I myself pray spontaneously; I think I should pray roughly like this:

I thank you, Lord, for my friends and those I work with.

Lead me to pray with joy, it is joy to share with you my life.

I pray with confidence, for you are at work in our hearts.

I desire to pray with love, my love enriched by your love.

Help me to pray that love may grow in the hearts of all men,

love, rich in knowledge and true discernment.

Lord, let me now remain still and receive your love.

And thank you for this time of quietness:

May your love and strength always be with us.

7

MEDITATION

And thou shalt follow me with thy affection
That from my words thy heart turn not aside.

DANTE

THREE young Japanese, who had almost finished their
studies for the Christian priesthood, were visiting one
of the less-known monasteries on Mount Athos. They
asked a staretz for spiritual advice. 'I'm only a simple
monk,' he protested, 'I can't help modern students like
yourselves.' But one of them begged: 'Father, teach us
meditation. We are thirsty for the Lord. Our professors
at home have lost contact with him, and they have
nothing authentic to give us.'

I can't tell you how many men and women have
asked me that same question; and so later in this chapter I will describe two methods of meditation which
have helped me, and I will try—as far as it is possible
—to give you a sample of each. One or other of these
methods may help you, or you may need to discover
some other way for yourself.

But I well understand the feelings of those Japanese
students, and also the problems of their professors in
this age of theological upheaval. You remember that
I told you how as a student for the ministry I lost my
faith; and how a priest gradually and patiently helped

me to find my way back to faith over successive intellectual hurdles.

Learning to Meditate

But the greatest thing which that priest did for me —or so it turned out in the long run—was that he brought me through to Christian meditation. He saw I was not ready for meditation at once. At that time I was still fairly agnostic; I certainly didn't know whether I should ever become a real believer, let alone be ordained. So I think his advice to me may be good for anyone who is seeking for light.

He began by recommending me while still an unbeliever to read, without any notes or commentary, a few verses of the New Testament each night. He suggested what passages I might start with. 'Never mind if they don't make much sense to you yet,' he said; 'just carry on. At least it shows you are seeking.' He encouraged me to try to find out what experience Jesus and the early Christians had had for such words to be written down. This went on for some months.

He led me through reflective reading, adapted first for an agnostic, next for a believer, and then on to meditation—three stages, which for me had no sharp frontiers.

Then he must have noticed my changing moods and my slowly growing faith. He began to talk to me about meditation; soon he taught me—as far as it can be taught—to meditate. I had my 'downs' as well as 'ups'. What helped me perhaps more than anything else was that he shared with me his own road to faith and in faith, as I would willingly do with you now.

To help me with my meditations he also encouraged me to make my first retreat. I went reluctantly. But that weekend of silence in that retreat-house literally did wonders for me. My annual retreats, since then, have been landmarks in my exploration. Many of my friends have found the same. If you haven't had this experience of a retreat, I hope you will do soon.

The Value of Meditation

Before describing ways of Christian meditation, let me tell you of two of its practical effects on my life. First, meditation has made Jesus for me, not only a great character of history, but someone who is *real* and *present* to me, through whom God meets me. Of course I am more aware of this truth at some times than at others, surface fogs can still cloud my vision, but deep down it is always there. 'You have not seen him,' a New Testament letter says, 'yet you love him.' Paul seems never to have met Christ in his life on earth; but, as the years went by, Paul could write: 'To me to live is Christ,' as a man might say of his beloved, 'She's my life.' The path to this presence of Christ, this love, this intimacy lies open to us all.

Secondly, meditation has convinced me that this love and power of God is focused through Christ on to me, on to you, to all men. We have to be awakened, and to help others to awake, to what—to Who—is there. He is available to, he is waiting for all the 'unwanted' and the 'inadequates' of our world. Meditation opens our eyes to God's possibilities *in them*. Here is hope for the transformation of society. Good legislation and adequate social care are important—and we must struggle for them—but to be effective they require also this dynamic of love, human and divine, in the world; it is irreplaceable. 'There is nothing love cannot face; there is no limit to its faith, its hope and its endurance.'

A few Distinctions

Meditation and contemplation have indeed a long and worldwide history. We've been left with a miniature babel of terms. I'm not much interested in labels: they can easily be misinterpreted. Moreover, men and women of prayer, like friends and lovers, don't like to analyse their affection and put it into technical terms. A brief—but I hope useful—glance at these terms, then, before telling you about my way of meditating so that you may start—or carry on—on your own.

We have divided prayer into 'giving-prayer' and 'receiving-prayer'. Older books have called them by, I think, misleading names, 'vocal prayer' and 'mental prayer'.

We can subdivide *'receiving-prayer'* into reflective reading, meditation and contemplation; of these three, the first is really prelude; the second, prayer predominantly of the intellect; and the third, prayer predominantly of the heart.

Older writers used to situate between meditation and contemplation a broad band of transition country, which in turn they further subdivided into three areas, never hard and fast divisions—affective prayer, prayer of the acts of the will, and the prayer of loving attention. I shall say nothing about them. You had better see these terms here, as you may come across them in your reading.

More important, many nineteenth and early twentieth-century writers used the word *contemplation* for prayer *only beyond* this transition country. They were following the terminology of St Teresa of Avila in the sixteenth century. Her younger contemporary, St John of the Cross, enlarged this term to include much of the transition country. Present-day writers in general, like some in the early Church, would bring the word 'contemplation' still further back to meet meditation.

All are agreed—we mentioned this first in chapter 1 —that contemplative prayer can come to quite ordinary people. We can look forward to it, we can open our hearts to receive it, and it always comes as a gift from God. The abnormal experiences of some of the mystics are no longer looked for as essential signs of contemplative prayer. Some say it is better without them! The real sign that our prayer is progressing is that our love is growing.

To complicate matters further, formerly methods of *meditation* used to be described in excessive detail. The first method I used happened to be 'Ignatian', called after St Ignatius of Loyola of the early sixteenth century. The next, which I stumbled upon, was 'Sulpician', after the name of a community of priests founded in the following century in the parish of St Sulpice in Paris. I was for some time happily ignorant of these old labels. These and other methods of meditation were explained for us afresh a generation or so ago by a book that made some of us too selfconscious in our meditations, as we tried to emulate one method or another—or even made up our own 'mix'. The bubble of selfconscious praying needs to be quickly and kindly pricked. The same priest, who had unknowingly given me such great help in my first retreat, did me this kindness. For a few years later I met him again; we talked about this book on methods and I asked him which of them he used himself. 'Oh, I just kneel down,' he replied, 'and hope for the best'—a typically English understatement from a real man of prayer. It taught me my lesson. In the life of prayer it is better not to try to categorise and classify.

Then a recent development in the West has been the spread of various new 'courses' on meditation and contemplation—many inspired by oriental spirituality. A widespread example is TM—transcendental meditation, introduced into the West by Maharishi Mahesh Yogi, who has developed it to help people of any or no religious faith. Many of his followers claim it has given them relief from tension, improved health and better working capacity. The Maharishi boldly invites medical and psychological testing of his methods.

They have made for us a further difficulty in terminology, for what they call transcendental meditation, a non-reflective state, is nearer to what Christians would nowadays call contemplation. Further, the followers of TM count on arriving at it without those years of regular reflecting and praying which we ourselves call meditation. They on the contrary expect rapid progress by skilled individual tuition, two periods of TM a day, careful training in posture and breathing and the use of an individually assigned *mantra*, a phrase often in Hindi and perhaps unintelligible, to be repeated again and again until the desired state is achieved.

What should we Christians think of all this? If TM really improves human wellbeing, we should be glad. The movement also shows that thousands of people are today unsatisfied with a purely materialistic way of life; they are searching for something more.

But there are differences between TM and traditional Christian methods. First, although a devout Hindu might use TM in a religious way, many of its followers in the West are probably looking only for direct personal benefits. In contrast we should be seeking primarily a deeper communion with God and only secondarily for relief from tension and similar benefits. Secondly, what the Christian meditates on matters to him supremely, namely, God, his creation and his self-disclosure in Christ; but the subject of his meditation does not concern the average follower of TM in that same way. Thirdly, the TM trainer and the Indian guru in general exercise—or are expected to exercise—a more authoritarian control over the trainee than the modern Christian spiritual adviser would agree to do. This is why Jung thought it wiser for Westerners to keep to their own traditions of spirituality. Fourthly, TM is, I think, a serious self-effort and self-culture. But Christian ways of prayer, in contrast, presuppose that we depend continuously and profoundly on the Spirit of God, given to us to dwell in our hearts.

First Way of Meditation

Now after these digressions let me try to describe meditation, which often develops out of our reflective reading. Again perhaps it may help you more if I write personally. But don't misunderstand me. I'm not good at meditation, though I should very much like to be. If for some reason I miss it, I feel it's like missing a meal, or rather more like missing a friend you were expecting. It's only gradually that meditation has come to mean so much to me. Yet if I have to miss my time of meditation on a particular day, I don't worry about it, because God is, I trust, steadily building up a relationship with me.

We may need to remind ourselves that meditation is the very opposite of day-dreaming. *Meditation is facing reality*; and, as we have seen, at the heart of reality is God's immense, unchangeable love, focused on each one of us, as surely as this divine love was focused on those Jesus met in his life. Awareness of this

93

fact should gradually become the perspective of our whole lives and service in the world.

The *aim of meditation* is that we may realise more and more deeply that we are loved by God and that we can, through his Spirit, respond with love both in our prayer and in the activities of our daily lives. We don't come to meditation primarily to learn more, or even to be 'reformed' ourselves. Yet this love of God concentrated on us will, if we are ready, change us—necessarily.

God's love is a transforming love. When our friends truly love us, they long that we should become our best selves, our true selves. But they do not set out heartlessly to 'reform' us, which might even produce the opposite effect. They long to see us transformed *through* loving. When Paul's love forced him to write a severe letter to the Christians at Corinth, he could say: 'How many tears I shed as I wrote it!' Jesus also, when he foresaw the fall of the Jerusalem he loved, wept over it. And so through our regular meditations we shall be changed by the Spirit of God—perhaps with pain—but certainly by love. But we come to our meditations, not primarily to see our faults which need to be corrected, but above all *to know we are loved* and through the Spirit of God to respond.

This is why meditation is tremendously important, and I think we simply must make time for it. First thing in the morning, as I have said, is certainly the best time. You might have opportunity for it in a lunch-time break, or in the early evening. Just before going to bed might suit you, but not me. I am tired, I can manage other kinds of prayer then, but if I tried to meditate I should fall off to sleep. And we need a place where we are not likely to be disturbed. Ten minutes might do, I suppose, when we are beginners. Let us make it as frequently as possible. Then it will probably grow on us. I now like, if possible, an hour each morning.

For many of us time is precious. We have to train ourselves to start at once. Let us not waste time asking ourselves: 'What passage shall I meditate on today?' This is why I still go on with my plan of reading the night before just a few verses from the bible. I go more or less straight through the gospels and through most of the epistles. I occasionally use parts of the Old Testament. You must make your own choice. You might even sometimes use some other book besides the bible. As I read, I usually pick out two or three phrases in the passage which look to me like possible 'leads in' for prayer. I let the passage just 'simmer' in my mind, when I go to bed, so that I am more ready for it in the morning, rather as we used to put the old-fashioned porridge on the night before and then it was ready and more digestible for breakfast.

When the actual time for meditation comes, I settle myself down, as I explained earlier in this book. Sometimes I picture our Lord with me; I usually say simply how glad I am to have this time of quiet; and I always ask for the Holy Spirit to help me. I might read the passage again, but nowadays I don't usually find it necessary.

Let me tell you roughly what I should do, if I were going to meditate on Jesus' prayer in Luke 10. 21–2. We notice that he first rejoices in the Holy Spirit and prays: 'I thank thee, Father, Lord of heaven and earth, for hiding these things from the learned and the wise, and revealing them to the simple.' He then adds: 'No one knows who the Son is but the Father, or who the

Father is but the Son, and those to whom the Son may choose to reveal him.' Something different may strike each of us as we read this passage. Let us each follow our own way. The juxtaposition of 'Father' with 'Lord of heaven and earth' might strike you. But the three things which most impress me are these. First, Jesus' prayer was a joyful prayer. Although I do not forget his hard prayer in Gethsemane, I guess that his prayers were fundamentally prayers of joy. Secondly, I would think that this joy used to spring out of his very special intimacy with the Father, of which he here speaks. It would be something like the joy close friends have in each other's company. Thirdly, I notice Jesus offers to others a share in this joyful intimacy of prayer—yet not to the learned, the over-confident, who know all the answers—but rather to the simple, who are open and eager to go forward. This brings to my mind those other words in John's gospel at the end of the seventeenth chapter about the love which the Father and the Son have for one another coming into our own hearts.

Then I should in a spirit of prayer reflect slowly on the first of my observations. I should turn my reflections at once into words of prayer. Meditation is not speculation but prayer. It is possible that at this moment Paul's words in his letter to the Philippians might occur to me: 'When I pray for you all, my prayers are always joyful.' I should probably now ask God to show me how my own prayers could be more genuinely joyful. Then I would pray spontaneously in my own way. Sometimes more words from the bible might spring to my lips, like the verse from the Psalms: 'My heart danceth for joy, and in my song will I praise him.' These words I might say slowly several times. This would not be shallow repetition. It would be more like lovers' words of affection and joy. And sometimes I might be quite still with a silence which to God is perhaps more eloquent than any words.

This might occupy nearly all my time of prayer. It is better to go over a little ground thoroughly and deeply than to try to cover too much ground. But if there were plenty of time, I should go back to my second observation and then afterwards perhaps to my third. Both of those observations are close to the word *Abba*; and they would certainly give me much food for prayer. All the reflections are intended to lead to prayer and love. It is this *flame of love* between God and ourselves which matters. It is not always emotional but it is always real. It is God's gift.

Near the end of the meditation I should try to think of something—perhaps quite small, like answering a friend's letter that day—to give my love some concrete expression. Then I should finish with a few words to God to express my gratitude and my confidence in him. I would take away with me some phrase of scripture, which as Dietrich Bonhoeffer said: 'should never stop ringing in your ears and working in you all the day long, just like the words of someone you love'.

I ought perhaps to tell you that, when I find I have too much material for my day's meditation, I keep it and use it the next day. Indeed I am finding—and much more recently—that I am happy to use the same material day after day. Bonhoeffer used to surprise his students by telling them to meditate on the same verses every day for a week; he said that this was the best way to learn to meditate and pray at depth.

Perhaps I could express my meditation on this prayer of Jesus in words like these:

Father, your Spirit dwells in my heart;
May he help me to enter into Jesus' way of praying;
May I too pray with thankfulness and joy.
Lord of heaven and earth, I may come to you as
   Abba, my Father.
I cannot know this if I am over-confident,
   but only if I am receptive and as open as a child.
What a joy, Father, to grow to know you as Jesus
   knows you;
   and to have in my life the love you have for him
   and he for you.

Second Way of Meditation

I went on with this kind of meditation (though not
without difficulties) for several years. Then quite by
chance I read about a second pattern of meditating.
This other method, then quite new to me, is summed
up in three phrases:

> Christ before me,
> Christ within me,
> Christ through me.

I thought I'd try, and it became the right path for me
for some years more.

Perhaps you might think that using the same three-
fold pattern day by day might become monotonous.
Some people might find it so. But I did not, because I
generally used it on a different passage of the bible. I
continued my practice of reading a few verses the night
before.

Let me illustrate how I might meditate in this way on
our Risen Lord's coming to the disciples after their
night of fishing on the lake (John 21. 1–17). I would
first remember that God has already sent his Spirit

into my heart. So I would ask that the Spirit would bring these events out of the past into the present—and make them not just past memories but present power. For Jesus himself is really present *before* me with all his love and power. As I quietly realise this, other New Testament passages may rise up within me and I may say them again and again slowly—this may take several minutes—'Lo, I am with you always'; 'Jesus Christ, the same yesterday and today and for ever.' Then I would try to remain before him for some time in silence, in thankfulness, in adoration, in love. So I would grasp that he is as close to me now as he was to Peter, when he asked him: 'Do you love me?' I remember that I, like Peter, have denied him in word and in action. I apologise, I tell him I wish to love him more deeply, to be loyal to him. He forgives me. I know he *has* to put this question to me, before he can entrust others to my care and love. And loving him first will help to prevent my care for them from being patronising, and my love for them from being possessive. But how can I offer to take upon myself these responsibilities?

Next I realise he wishes to dwell *within* me. What a marvel this is! As I try to hold on to this fact other verses come to me: 'Abide in me, and I in you'; 'Through faith may Christ dwell in your hearts in love.' And I remember also my holy communion. 'Whoso eats my flesh and drinks my blood dwells continually in me, and I in him.' Quietly and slowly I try to grasp that, because Christ dwells in me, his strength and his joy and his love must be in me. I am still. I try not to be anxious about all the work waiting to be done. I have his strength. 'In quietness and in confidence shall be your strength.' Christ's love too is within me; then why should I keep asking myself: 'How shall I be able to cope with So-and-so? Why should I be so tense? Why not let his love flow through me? Why not let his love change me gradually from inside?' And his joy also is already within me: 'that my joy may be in you and your joy complete'. Of course I shall have things to depress me like everyone else, disappointments, partings and all the rest. But underneath them all is his joy, a sparkling spring of joy. Paul too knew this. 'Sorrowful,' he wrote—and if we aren't sometimes sorrowful, we aren't human—'yet,' he adds, 'always rejoicing.'

Christ before me, Christ within me, and then Christ *through* me. He wishes to go through me today everywhere I go—to my desk to prepare that article, to those students who have asked to see me, to that chore that has to be done. The question is not: 'What must I try to do for Christ?' but 'What does Christ want to bring there and there and there through me?' It may not be words. It certainly is love.

Then towards the end of my meditation I just want to be quiet, alone with him—and then say 'Thank you'; and 'You'll be with me.' Sometimes at the very end I find it a help to write down a few words. Dag Hammarskjöld used to do this, so did Charles de Foucauld. But they are words just for our own eyes and his and nobody else's. Dag Hammarskjöld called his words *Markings*, and these can be our 'markings' on our journey of exploration. Often in our lives it helps us to look back and to be reminded of these moments with the Lord. Many times they become encouragements for us to press on further. They have been for me.

But I mustn't give a false impression. I am very far from succeeding in my meditations and prayers, but I go on trying. Something seems to have been happening these last few years. I don't know how long it will go on. Perhaps something else quite unexpected may happen. It is like building up real human love and trust. It takes time.

Let me now try to summarise this meditation on the Risen Jesus meeting his disciples by the lake; you might like to use it:

Lord, help me by your Spirit really to pray;
    and to know you belong to the present, not to the past.
You are now *before* me as you were by the lake.
You ask me if I truly love you;
    unless I do, I cannot love others, as you do.
Come, Lord, and dwell *in* my heart through faith.
And go, Lord, *through* me wherever I go today,
    bringing to others strength, love and joy.

8

CONTEMPLATION

Come to me with your heart, and I will give you my eyes.

ARAB PROVERB

THE sparkle and the daily walk together—that is the life of friendship and love, isn't it?—and that is the life of prayer. Many books on the life of prayer talk entirely about the daily walk together, our daily faithfulness to God; and rather dull it sometimes sounds. But there is also the sparkle, the 'high moments', the peak-experiences.

'High Moments'

Once I was at a conference in Rome and I was taken to the Church of St Peter's Chains and there in front of me was that stupendous sculpture of Moses by Michelangelo. Although I had seen plenty of reproductions of it, none of them had given me any real sense of its majestic strength. Maybe this figure does not speak to everyone, it might not have spoken to me at some other time. That day I was in the right mood. Anyway the coincidence of the moment and the masterpiece did something to me.

First, it gripped me, it held me enthralled, it took me out of myself. I lost all sense of the passing of time. I was inwardly silent and open.

Then there was conveyed to me—I can't say how—a sense of wonder at what man is—a sense not only of his physical strength, but of his spiritual strength; of man as he is capable of becoming, of man who is answering to a call and challenge beyond himself—of man in communion with God; man called and sent into this world by God. I do not know how long this was going on, but I felt something immense pouring into me; I was not only looking, I was receiving something.

Next I began to feel something awakening in me. It was like waking up to love. I wanted to respond, to respond to love, to trust increasingly in the One who had empowered—who had sent Moses, that man of God, to bring something new to his people and to the world. I felt in a new and indescribable way that I too had been spoken to, had been called and was being called still further to become a real Christian, to be really a priest at the service of others. I was responding—and responding in a power that was not my own.

When at last I came out of the church into the bright sunlight of the streets of Rome, people looked different. The tourist and the waiter, the taxi-man as well as the nun were, I saw, far more than they dreamed of. Every one of them—every one of us—has an inner capacity for that fellowship with God which Moses had—a fellowship that gives purpose, strength and love. Here is hope for our troubled world. I felt I was being renewed—renewed for service that very day, and for the years to come.

These 'high moments' come to many people—perhaps most often through the wonders of nature. You will remember Wordsworth's *Lines above Tintern Abbey*:

                    And I have felt
A presence that disturbs me with the joy
Of elevated thoughts; a sense sublime
Of something far more deeply interfused,
Whose dwelling is the light of setting suns,
And the round ocean, and the living air,
And the blue sky, and in the mind of man.

The moments come, I believe, to nearly all of us. How many, for instance, have been inwardly moved by the crash of a wave on a beach, as I mentioned right at the beginning of this book. These moments replenish us. They speak to heart as well as mind. They help to bring us to inner harmony. But we are, for various reasons, shy to speak of them. There are, I am sure, many mute, inglorious Wordsworths.

But I must not be mute, for I am convinced that these experiences can open up the lives and prayers of ordinary people like ourselves. Such unforgettable moments have come to me through nature in nearly all her moods. I remember once, while I was camping by a lake, how I watched the pale orange light that slowly heralded the dawn, next the beams of gold, and then the rising sun reflected in the still, silent water; another time, when I was both shaken and exalted by the fierceness of nature in the power and majesty of a thunderstorm in a mountain valley; and again, how when lying on a hillside I felt strangely at one with the wind stirring the long grass around me, with the sap rising up in the blades, with all the hidden sources of the life of nature—and inwardly I knew that all this manifold life had its deep spring in the Spirit of the Lord. Each time in a different way, my heart stopped,

I marvelled, I received something. I responded and wanted to share it with others.

But these 'high moments' do not come only among the beauties of nature, or in churches, or in art galleries or at concerts. They come in the ordinary run of daily life—through an act of courage seen in a busy street, through an act of kindness done in a hospital ward, the light in the eyes of a child, the smile of a friend. We see them if we are alert. We are moved, we are opened, we wish to do something to express our appreciation. Marvel is, as we said, prior to inspired action.

All these moments are precious, good in themselves, like music, friendship and love—but also they can have lasting consequences. Wordsworth in the same poem said:

> In this moment there is life and food
> For future years.

Moments and their Consequences

These moments humanise us. Never were they needed more than today. It is true we live in a wonderful epoch, and the achievements of our science are amazing. Yet, because our world goes all out for efficiency and speed, it is dehumanising us, pressurising us, hurrying us into treating men and women as 'types' rather than persons, because we haven't, we think, time—or love—for more.

I believe that if I—I do not know about you—am going to keep truly human, let alone Christian, I need somehow to *open* myself to similar *humanising* moments, if possible every day. You see the importance of this. But how can it happen?

Let's think, each of us, if we can, of one of those

special moments which have come to us. We remember we were elated for the moment. But what next? We could then make one or other of two mistaken steps. We could easily either let the experience slip away unremembered, unpondered upon, perhaps even wondering whether there was 'anything in it'; or alternatively we could try artificially to 'build up to it' again and recapture it for ourselves, and then be discouraged if we failed. Neither of those two ways of treating that experience is satisfactory. The realistic way to treat these moments is, I am convinced, as 'Pisgah experiences', like Moses climbing and seeing from Mt Pisgah the direction in which the people were to journey on in the future. Our 'high moments' are real; they are something to be grateful for; but they are more the beginning than the goal of our journey; but most important, our 'high moments' are *invitations and encouragements to journey on and on and on.*

So these 'high moments' should invigorate us to press on with our journey of exploration. They should encourage us, in particular, to make the best possible use of our daily times of 'receiving-prayer'—reflective reading, meditation, contemplative praying. The sparkle should illuminate that essential daily walk.

A friend of mine, who had read what I had written in earlier books about these 'high moments', said that he could appreciate them—in fact he had them himself—but then he went on to ask: 'But what kind of connection can there be between those moments and my own rather mundane daily prayers?' In fact how is the sparkle related to the daily walk together? Let us look together at that question.

We cannot live entirely on 'high moments'. We see a similarity in music. The musician and the singer have their 'high moments' when in a concert 'it really comes off'. They then play, they sing, as they say, better than they knew how. But behind those moments and preparing for those moments are months and years of slogging practice—though, sometimes, even in the practice itself a joy and a flash of inspiration breaks through.

There is a closer similiarity in friendship and love. We have special moments of unforgettable wonder. These stand out in the setting of years of steady, and not always easy, companionship. Yet even in those more ordinary times there are moments which sparkle with an anticipation of something more wonderful yet to come.

Journeying On

We are glimpsing the possibilities ahead. But are we —we, ordinary men and women—aiming too high? I don't think so. We have seen that we have the basic aptitude for it. We just need steady encouragement and discerning advice. I am writing the whole of this book to encourage you. I would like now to give three pieces of advice for this part of the journey.

First, although we shall have joys on the way, we should not *seek* for moving 'spiritual experiences' for ourselves. In fact in our 'high moments' and often in our contemplative praying we are taken out of ourselves, we are not concerned with ourselves, we are absorbed in looking at God and at how he has disclosed himself. We seek God and not our own satisfaction. Indeed this contemplative prayer should progressively cleanse all our praying and all our service of others from self-seeking.

Secondly, we should try not to be deterred by the possible painfulness of this cleansing from our self-centredness. It is God's love that cleanses us. We accept the cleansing through our growing love. And it will eventually help us to love more. Of this kind of progress in our prayer Douglas Steere, an American Quaker friend of mine, has said: 'it is an acknowledgement of our finitude, our need, our openness to be changed, our readiness to be surprised—yes astonished —by the "beams of love"'.

Thirdly, most of us will, I think, come to contemplative prayer through meditation. But there are nowadays men and women who can make nothing of meditation, but can be guided fairly quickly to contemplative praying. And St John of the Cross himself said—though I think to those who had been accustomed to meditation—'When a spiritual person cannot meditate, let him learn to be still in God, fixing his loving attention upon him, in the calm of his understanding.'

And we all know what was told of that French peasant who on his way home after a day's work used to sit quite still in the village church with his eyes fixed on the altar. When someone asked him what he was doing all that time he replied simply: 'The Lord looks at me and I look at him.' The peasant had 'arrived'— without any of our systematic preparations. Contemplative praying is experienced, as real love is, *only* as a gift and not as a result of our own clever use of spiritual techniques. 'The Spirit blows where he wills.'

Pointers towards Contemplative Praying

I find it impossible to say just where I am on this journey. I am not good at prayer. I wish I were. Perhaps like others I go backwards and forwards. You may have sensed from what I said about my attempts to meditate, that I am on the move. If so, I think you are right. It is developing into something like a small daily Michelangelo experience. I do not mean it is always a moving emotional experience, but I think I can say it is becoming a sparkle, a moment of insight, of love. I've had three pointers to encourage me to go on. Possibly you may have had similar indications.

First, I have had these 'high moments', these 'Pisgah experiences'. They were nothing very extraordinary, but they pointed me on. I think most people have them —though, as I said, they do not talk about them much. By-the-way, if nothing at all like this has ever happened to you, don't worry, still less don't be discouraged. When God gives these experiences to people, he does not give them just for their own benefit, but for everybody's benefit. It is the same when the New Testament says the gifts of the Spirit are given to us, not only for ourselves, but for the good of the whole body of God's people. Or again on another level we are glad that some men and women are poets and musicians, sculptors and painters—even if we are not—because it tells us something of the wonderful potentialities of our common human nature, and also that there is a trace of some skill in us, even if only in embryo. I know I am more of a man because Shakespeare became Shakespeare—and because Teresa became Teresa.

Secondly, my meditative praying was simplifying in the direction of contemplative praying. This again is quite common. I found myself reasoning about the passages less, and picturing the events of the gospels very much less. And let us remember that this use of the imagination and of the intellect is always preparation for prayer, rather than prayer itself. It is like collecting and arranging sticks and twigs in preparation for a bonfire—important in their way—but the real thing doesn't happen until you put a match to it and have a good blaze. Let me say once again: the essence of prayer is the blaze of love between God and you.

When we have really come to know and love God—perhaps after years of meditation—his love remains in our heart, like glowing embers. And then blowing on the embers is enough to bring them to flame; you don't have to go out and collect some new wood. A better analogy is the difference between meeting an acquaintance and a very close friend, both after a long absence. With the acquaintance you have, as we say, to pick up the links, say what you have both been doing, before you settle down to real and serious conversation. This picking up of the links corresponds to the using of the imagination and the reflecting in prayer. But these preliminaries are not necessary with your close friend, indeed they are rather a waste of time; you are *en rapport* at once.

A similar change was coming over my use of words, as it does with other people. When we first meditate we usually say many words, like the early weeks of a friendship. As time goes on in meditation and in friendship we may speak less and mean more. In contemplative praying we often repeat slowly some well-loved phrase; just as lovers can say and are happy to say and to hear the words, 'I love you' over and over again—words which not only express but deepen love. And often in contemplative praying, as in love, silence can say more than any words.

Let us not be impatient with our progress, provided that we are trying to be open and receptive.

These simplifications come quickly for some people. For me they came slowly—perhaps they will for you.

They often come gradually—but they really come—when we deeply realise how immensely we are loved by God. Only when we *know* that we are loved like this —and it is true also of human friendship and love— can we blossom out into our real selves, the men and women God meant us to become—and, of course, only then can we do our best service for others and for the transformation of the world.

Thirdly, pointers often come from books we read, and books seem to turn up, or are recommended to us, just about when we need them. The third pointer for me has been a book which has recently come into my hands. It is really intended for men and women further on than I am; some of it is quite beyond me; but it is now giving me valuable hints about the way ahead. It is called *The Cloud of Unknowing*, by an unknown author of the fourteenth century.

The book is gold out of the furnace of his own experience. He writes with charm, simplicity and directness. He is no mean scholar, a translator of Dionysius the Areopagite, a Syrian man of prayer of the fifth century. He has a sense of humour and makes gentle fun of the affectations of pseudo-religious people. Some speak, he says, with such gesticulations that you might think that 'they are swimming an ocean'; and others look so awe-struck that you might think they are 'stargazing as if they want to get past the moon'. He maintained that, contrary to this, true contemplation should give man 'the knack of being at home with everyone he talks to'. He speaks of the importance of reading or hearing the bible. He thinks that reflective meditation is the indispensable preparation for and the door into this simpler contemplative prayer. He realises that readers may find parts of his book difficult. He suggests they read it two or three times. Then if it does not suit their temperament, let them leave it alone; and, he says, with the advice of a wise guide, find another way more suitable to them.

I have learnt much from *The Cloud*, as it is usually called. I cannot go all the way with the author. His concept of God, which he derived from Dionysius the Areopagite, is remote and highly abstract and needs to be balanced by the *Abba*, Father, of the gospels and by the divine Spirit who dwells in our hearts by faith. He also seems to me to speak of our love too much as an effort of the will—again and again he uses the phrase 'the naked intent of the will'—and not as the response of our whole personality.

Simple Contemplative Praying

But let me now try to say how my prayer is developing. I am rather apprehensive about doing this. This is no standard way of praying. I feel such an amateur. And I don't know what other changes may come over my prayer. I seem on the edge of something—I don't know what. But other men and women who talk to me about their prayers seem to be in about the same situation. So it is quite ordinary, not at all special.

I continue to read my few verses from the New Testament each night. But often in the morning my own mind turns like a magnet to great passages where Jesus has often met with me before, those treasured meditations on the Lord's words in John's gospel, chapters 14–17, the first three chapters of the letter to the Ephesians and most of all to the fourth chapter of the first letter of John: those incomparable words 'God is love'; 'The love I speak of is not our love of God, but the love he has shown to us in sending his Son'; 'We love, because he loved us *first*,' and 'He who loves God loves his brother also.' What I am going to say about my own present 'receiving-prayer' I will base on that last passage. You will also see that I am beginning to learn from *The Cloud of Unknowing*.

My own time of prayer—and this is nearly always in the morning—has normally a fourfold sequence like my Michelangelo experience. First, there is the time of settling down and looking to God; for this I often say a few times quite slowly: 'In God we live' and 'God is love'. Often distractions come. Sometimes people I have met or know well come into my mind. If so, I intercede briefly for them, and this is no real hindrance to my prayer, because my desire is fundamentally that they too should be held more securely in the divine love. But sometimes fears, worries, muddles, failings, come to my memory also. This is not the time to analyse them, the author of *The Cloud* tells us, nor, he says, to make a detailed confession—there is a time for that, but not now. I simply say: 'Lord, you know all this, and yet still you love me.'

Secondly—and most important of all—I try to keep my attention on that divine love which ceaselessly pours upon us, like heat radiated from the sun; and often the words run through my mind—no, more deeply than that—'not our love of God, but the love he has shown us', shown us eternally in Christ. I must try, at least in this part of my praying, to give my whole heart to this. I must let all else, if I can, sink for a time into what our author calls the cloud of forgetting, the cloud beneath me. I must try—and he tells me it may sometimes be hard work—to concentrate entirely on God and his love. Sometimes—for many people, often—God, who is there, seems to have hidden himself in the cloud above us, the cloud of unknowing. 'Clouds and darkness are round him,' as one of our psalms says. And we cannot *at this stage* break through to him by our reflecting and reasoning. 'He may well be loved, but not thought. By love God can be caught and held, but by thinking never,' this book says, and it goes on: 'Strike that thick cloud of unknowing with the *sharp dart of longing love,* and on no account whatever think of giving up.' We do so in complete silence, or perhaps by repeating a phrase slowly without any attempted reasoning about it. I myself like to use just a name—perhaps *Abba,* Father, or Jesus, or Holy Spirit. Our author says: 'The shorter the word the better, being more like the working of the Spirit. A word like "God" or "love". Choose which you like, or perhaps some other, so long as it is of one syllable.'

Thirdly, I know I must try to respond as deeply and as widely as I can. 'We love, because he loved us first.' This response I may express in some words of scripture which come spontaneously to my lips or else in my own words—or more often in silence, because love of this kind is beyond words. It is the love of our hearts, but it is more. It is with all our heart and mind, soul and strength, that Jesus invites us to love.

Then finally this love, if it is deep, will by its very nature overflow as real love between a husband and wife overflows to their family and neighbours. 'He who loves God loves his brother also. He who lives in love lives in God and God lives in him.' So almost always I end this time of receiving-prayer with thanksgiving and also with praying just for three or four people in depth, so that these people will, I trust, share with me in some of the blessing of love which God has given to me. *The Cloud of Unknowing* reminds us that those who are united to God by love are by that same love united to one another.

If for some reason at the start of this receiving-prayer I feel lazy or disinclined to begin or to carry on, I think of those I wish very much to pray for and consider that they too may lose something, if I fail to persevere. That usually is stimulus enough for me.

To try to make clearer what this kind of prayer is for me at least for the present, and to show how it runs into intercession, I venture with some hesitation to share with you the kind of words I often use. Of course words in print—you will understand—are inadequate for anything so personal.

Lord, you are always sustaining me,
    like the air around me and within me.
Here I begin to realise your immense, unchangeable love,
    and to receive it into my heart.
And I respond to you with love,
    through your Holy Spirit dwelling in me.
I draw into this love, which is yours and mine,
    those I pray for, care for and love.
So may love this day inspire and gladden,
    refresh and strengthen them.

Simple receiving-prayer of this kind could through the Holy Spirit revitalise our style of living, our whole range of praying and our serving the world.

Contemplating and Living

In those *Lines above Tintern Abbey* Wordsworth wrote: 'We see into the life of things.' Contemplative praying should lead to contemplative living, because we are starting to look quietly right into the life of things. Alan Ecclestone says: 'Contemplative living is really a matter of learning to see, and to see with new-opened eyes the world in which we live.'

This kind of seeing, a consequence of contemplative praying, means not—at least consciously—imposing our preconceived ideas on what we see and hear. We let people and things be what they are. We respect them. Perhaps this is what a Roman Catholic nun of rather an untraditional type meant when she said to me in the States a year or two ago: 'to be human involves being contemplative'. The depth of our communication with God begins to mould our communication with others. Our own inner attitudes towards them change and a door is opened to the growth of understanding and to love-in-action. 'Come to me with your heart, and I will give you my eyes.' All this might be the small beginnings of another kind of society for us.

Contemplating and Praying

This rather elementary kind of contemplative receiving-prayer may revitalise our whole range of praying. It can begin in small ways.

We may find that our moments of prayer in the course of a busy day will be less often appeals for help, little intercessions, or expressions of gratitude, and rather more often tiny pools of contemplative silence. I remember often looking at a picture in a house where I sometimes stay—there under a wide sky with wisps of clouds the waves of the sea are breaking on flat black rocks, not violently but with a fine white spray, and the rocks themselves are glistening with innumerable trickles of water. That picture can set me off.

Dom Cuthbert Butler says that it is quite normal for these 'moments of contemplation' to come to us during the day and also during our usual times of prayer. He mentions particularly the minutes of silence in church after receiving holy communion. He says we should treasure—that is his own word—all these times, and just rest in them, until we find our attention waning into mere emptiness or into other important concerns. I myself find I am now sometimes drawn to say the Lord's prayer very slowly with a kind of contemplative pause between the petitions, and I was much encouraged when I noticed John Dalrymple speaking of taking fifteen minutes to pray this prayer.

I expect that the link between intercession and contemplation is becoming clear to you. John Baker has many wise things to say about the life of prayer in the latter part of his book, *The Foolishness of God*, and he specially stresses the need of a contemplative attitude when we intercede. 'When we pray for others, we shall see that the most important requirement by far is inner calmness and tranquillity. Our task is to hold the awareness of them in the still centre of our being, to unite our love for them with God's love, in the quiet but total confidence that he will use our love to help to bring about the good in them which we both desire. In technical terms, therefore, intercession is a form of that kind of prayer known as "contemplation".'

Its link with thanksgiving is even clearer. We have a similar experience sometimes when we thank a close friend; we say: 'Thank you for that and that and that'; then we feel inwardly impelled to go on to add: 'And thank you above all for just being yourself. You are so wonderful.' So in our prayers when we have plenty of time, we can go on and on thanking God, beginning with what is most real and precious to us; and sometimes this impulse of thankfulness sweeps us on further to praise, adoration and the silent contemplation of God in his unceasing, overflowing love.

Simple, receptive contemplative praying can be a wonderful preparation for worship together. I realised this once when I was staying at Taizé. The bells rang about half an hour before the evening service. We gradually collected. Leisurely we settled down. We sat still, fascinated by the play of colour as the light of the setting sun shone obliquely through the windows and watching the flicker of the ring of candles suspended high above the altar. It was this contemplative stillness which enriched—I almost said which 'made'—that evening worship.

We usually think of this simple contemplative praying as personal and individual, but it can also be an experience deeply shared. I remember leading a day's seminar for young people on eucharistic worship in a house above Santa Barbara in California, overlooking the Pacific. We had worked hard all day, studying the structure of the eucharist, preparing the scripture passages, practising the music. We decided to make our eucharist as contemplative as we could, with several periods of silence together. It was a warm evening and we celebrated the eucharist in the garden. The sun was just sinking into the ocean, with the sky gold, then fiery red, then purple. After receiving holy communion I said quietly: 'May Christ through faith dwell in your hearts in love.' For a whole half hour we were just so glad to be still with our hearts full of gratitude and adoration.

But contemplation does much more than this for our worship. No one has made this clearer than Thomas Merton. I am going to quote him a good deal in this chapter. What he says can only be understood if you remember what he was. He knew agnosticism from inside when he was a student at Columbia, New York. He spent most of his adult life in a Trappist monastery. Significantly he wrote: 'The monk leaves the world only to listen to the deepest voices that he has left behind.' Monk, contemplative at heart, as he was, he touched life deeply and widely through his prayers, his friendships and his writing. He particularly felt on his pulses the problem of war, the social struggles and the dialogue with oriental spirituality. And it was at Bangkok in 1968 that he died through an accident at a conference, at the age of fifty-three.

Thomas Merton saw the importance of contemplation in itself, but he also saw in it a *safeguard* to prevent worship from becoming over-fussy in detail, shallowly aesthetic and indeed remote from life. 'Without the spirit of contemplation in all our worship— that is to say without the adoration and love of God above all, for his own sake, because he is God—the liturgy will not nourish a really Christian apostolate based on Christ's love and carried out in the power of the Spirit.'

Contemplation and Serving the World

Living contemplatively does not mean that we become mild 'Yes men', passive non-reformers in the world. We listen to others first, remembering that God should be in our silence and in our speech, and then we may have to say a very decided 'No' or 'Yes'. St Teresa, who was a contemplative if ever there was one, after her own conversion in middle age, earned the name of gad-about, travelling in a rocking, creaking wagon and staying at bug-infested inns, as she went out reforming her Carmelite order and founding new houses—for the renewal of the Church in the world. St Vincent de Paul, getting up each morning for silent prayer at four o'clock, initiated forms of social service in a war-ridden France and was listened to in the highest circles of church and state.

Thomas Merton too, as we have just seen, had a deep concern for the world. He firmly believed he himself had a contribution to make. But he knew he could not make it, unless he pressed further and further on in this exploratory journey of prayer. He may be far in front of us, but we are on the same journey. There are plenty of joys and adventures. But there are deserts to be crossed. Sometimes it may be dark. Thomas Merton met men and women, even a long way on their journey, who in the darkness seemed to have lost their faith. Perhaps it was that their old over-simplified concepts of God had to dissolve as part of their purification. He told them to take courage to face this 'experience of being apparently without faith *in order to grow in faith*'. He knew he must persevere himself, and he wrote:

> May my burns burn and ravens eat my flesh
> If I forget thee, contemplation.

He was convinced that we need a contemplative spirit if we are to struggle for the transformation of the world. Contemplation will keep us awake to the twin opposite temptations which will face us there— Frère Roger, you remember, alerted the Council of Youth to them at Taizé—either to impose arrogantly our ideas on others or else to make specious compromises with worldly men. How to preserve this contemplative spirit in our tasks in the world I will return to in our concluding chapter. But before you put down this chapter on contemplation, would you quietly reflect on these further encouraging words of Thomas Merton: 'Without contemplation the Church will be reduced to being the servant of cynical and worldly powers, no matter how hard her faithful may protest that they are fighting for the Kingdom of God. Without contemplation and interior prayer the Church cannot fulfil her mission to transform and save mankind.'

9

PRAYING TOGETHER

*What is most intimate and essential for me is
the presence and love of others.*

ROGER GARAUDY

No one can guess now what your exploration of prayer
may bring. You will know, you will discover for yourself. You may perhaps need times of solitude. Mother
Julian of Norwich in medieval England and Charles
de Foucauld at Tamanrasset in the Sahara in our century are clear—though extreme—examples of this need
to go apart in order to explore. But even in their solitude, they were not lonely. They knew they were praying in the one Spirit, and through the Spirit were
united to the whole people of God. Bonhoeffer, alone
in his prison, rising early for prayer, knows he is one
with his parents and his fiancée. 'At 6-oo a.m. I like to
read psalms and hymns, think of you all, and know you
are thinking of me.' In the seminary of the Confessing
Church at Finkenwalde he had stressed the same thing
when he taught his theological students, soon to be
scattered in the dangers of Nazi persecution and in the
coming war, that in prayer they would be always linked
invisibly to one another and to the Risen Christ, 'who
ever lives to make intercession for us'.

How vital it is to remember this fact! Yet there are
many ways in which we might be helped by praying

informally in the *visible* company of others. Many of us may need to share in different groups at different stages of our exploring and praying. Groups grow, become smaller, re-form in different patterns. Variety and flexibility are natural, since our work or our studies keep us moving about and also our needs are continually changing. Personally I don't see our sharing in this kaleidoscope of groups as a substitute for our belonging to the universal Church; but, rather, I see the great Church as the background and hidden support for these changing groups.

Difficulties with Groups

But I know people who pray a good deal alone and join in church worship, and who are still reluctant to join any informal prayer-group. We should try to understand them and why they hesitate.

They are against—and so am I—pressure put on anyone to join a prayer-group. If someone had tried at one stage of my life to pressurise me, he might easily have put me off for good. Nor, I think, are groups very useful, unless their members, diverse as they often are, grow into a sense of belonging to one another. Any group could be spoilt by having too many new members at once. The choice of leader seems to me crucial. He needs the skill of leading unobtrusively. He should know how to deal with the over-selfconfident as well as how to give encouragement to the shy. He must see that prayers don't become oblique exhortations, and particularly watch that no one tries to make others feel guilty or inadequate. He should also help people not to think, while they are praying, of the impression they are making on their fellow-members—or at least to grow up out of such an attitude. He needs to see that intercessions are discreet—prayer-groups have been called 'gossip-shops'—and that the impression isn't given that by some kind of prayer-pressure we can extract answers out of a reluctant God. There is, as I have said, an important place for perseverance in prayer, but that is not to bring God into action, but rather to put us in the right frame of mind to be able to receive the blessings God wishes to give. If these things were watched, more people might gain from praying together informally in one of the many possible ways.

The Value of Groups

Even if there are dangers, or rather abuses, in these groups, how very many good things there are about them! Many of us have been brought up to see prayer as essentially a one-to-one relationship with God. This has indeed gone so deep with some of us that—though we may make some verbal concession to other points of view—in our hearts we really regard the corporate worship of the Church as the synchronisation of individual praying together in the same building.

But in the New Testament there is that other model for our prayer-relationship with God, the one that 'solitaries' too are aware of: that when we truly pray as individuals, we are praying together as members of the one Body of Christ, helped by the one Holy Spirit. So when I pray, what the Holy Spirit is doing in me is linked to what he is doing in my fellow-Christians. And the Holy Spirit's help is never only for our individual good alone but also for the building up of the Body of Christ. We should try to share together in an awareness of God in the Body of Christ through his Spirit. Further, if our group includes some who would not wish to call themselves Christians, we should still remember that the New Testament says that the Logos, the Word of God, enlightens every man, leads our efforts and is our real, if unseen, bond. So our attention should always be centred on the Lord, and those we are praying with be just beyond our conscious horizon. At the end of our prayer we should be—to use a biblical phrase—'united in heart and soul'.

But let the pendulum swing too far from this one-to-one model of prayer, and we may find ourselves even in times of worship and praise, being more conscious of others than of God: in some ultra-communal eucharists, for instance, the aim may be to promote fraternal love, but real prayer is being given a push-off.

For all real prayer—and there can be no rigid boundaries between liturgical prayer, informal praying together and individual prayer, for they enrich one another—is fundamentally receiving God's love, responding to it in the power of the Spirit, and so sharing it with others.

Kinds of Groups

Not only because we are at different stages in our exploration, but because we are temperamentally different, many sorts of prayer-groups are needed. Again, may I share my experience with you, and make a few suggestions? A membership of six to ten seems about right for most groups. Usually we have met weekly or every two weeks, apart from holiday periods. Sometimes we have gone on only for a few months; sometimes, happily, for several years. A helpful group, I have found, is one that is really sensitive to one another's needs and to the leading of the Spirit of God. So far I have never found very appealing names for the main types of groups that have helped me—but let's not be put off by that. And these various kinds of groups can shift, change and almost merge into one another.

Dialogue Groups

Dialogue groups include believers, non-believers and some who would rather not classify themselves. The underlying aim of those I have belonged to has been to study man and his needs, including—even the non-believers were prepared to admit—his more 'spiritual' needs. We avoided the cut-and-thrust of argument, which is proper and enjoyable in a debating society. We soon came to know one another well enough to share frankly our own experiences and convictions. None of us claimed to be experts and none to be *mere* learners. We all learned a great deal; and two or three, I think, took a step towards faith. Of course no pressure was put on anybody. We decided to have at all our meetings short periods of shared silence, usually ten to fifteen minutes, although in each group some used this time for reflection rather than prayer. A most valuable member of one of these groups was a psychiatrist who was an agnostic. He helped me and others to make useful distinctions about things we often confuse. He could not himself on intellectual grounds pray in any normally accepted way, but he spoke of the positive rôle which prayer has in many believers' lives. True prayer is no flight from life, he said, not even a cushioning against its more painful knocks; instead it could help people to face reality, to find themselves, and to make better relationships with others.

In another of these groups contemplation seemed as interesting to non-believers as to believers. We there described contemplation as quietly and leisurely opening ourselves to the great reality, however differently we might each conceive that reality. We all saw the folly of looking too hurriedly at everyone and everything through our own presuppositions. We thoroughly discussed the German saying, *Werde was du bist* – 'become what you are'. We all agreed, unbelievers and believers alike, that contemplation could be a real help in this essential process. Another agnostic, high up in university administration and extremely busy, said in this group that he must somehow make time for this sitting inwardly still; and though he could not, he said, pray contemplatively, he would try to live contemplatively.

Meditation Groups

So many people have told me recently of the help they have received from meditation groups of very varied types. I haven't yet led a group through a series of meditation sessions. But when conducting schools of prayer I have often given an instruction on meditative and contemplative prayer, and have sometimes followed it by a kind of conducted meditation. In many places this seems to have been the kind of help people have long been looking for. It is very elementary. I begin by helping them each to find some suitable posture which leads them to what I paradoxically call a 'relaxed alertness' and to settle down for this meditative prayer. Then slowly, with considerable pauses, I lead a prayer based on a biblical passage I have just spoken about. I suggest that they might like to offer these thoughts to God in almost wordless prayer, or else continue this same prayer to God silently in their own way. Next I usually give them a short phrase, which they can, if they wish, repeat slowly and let somehow seep down into their whole being. I ask them to try all the time to focus themselves much more on God and his love than on the words and their precise meaning. After some time of silence, perhaps five or ten minutes, I give them a similar phrase, or sometimes the first phrase expanded. Then, rather more silence. Finally, I try to draw the threads together with another short prayer said slowly—linked with the themes of thanksgiving and confidence. Afterwards people have told me that they have had a sense of that 'shared awareness of God'. And it has given them an impetus to try to bring into their ordinary daily lives this quiet, receptive waiting on God.

In some schools of meditation similar methods are used for therapeutic purposes—either for some specific healing or for alleviation of stress in the person meditating, or else to help this person to intercede more deeply for someone else who is suffering. There is evidence of emotional and also physical healing given in these ways. But I myself would prefer to regard this healing as secondary to the direct purpose of this prayer: namely, to let the Holy Spirit open us up to God's immense, unceasing love, to help us to respond and so share this love with those we meet in daily life and with those for whom we intercede. I am also convinced of the importance of the laying-on of hands on the sick with prayer, and I could tell of great benefits which have come in this way. For these blessings we should indeed thank God—but not, I think, talk too much about them, as Jesus in the gospels told people not to speak about his miraculous healings. For much as we seek God's gifts, we must surely be seeking even more the Giver himself.

Koinonia Groups

I have belonged to several groups which could not have been described exactly as meditation groups, or dialogue groups, or intercession groups, or bible-study groups. So we chose and kept as a title *koinonia* group, from the Greek Testament word which means 'sharing together a common life, whose source is in God'. The French call them *communautés de base*. We wished to share together the deep things of life, including as deep an experience of prayer as possible. There was no set programme in these groups. But let me describe roughly what used to happen. We normally began with a drink and informal conversation about things that had happened since our last meeting. Then the host—we usually met in one another's houses—or the chairman of the group would call us to order. We had fairly precise times when the meeting began and officially finished. Although we occasionally studied books about prayer, like Fénelon's *Letters* or C. S. Lewis' *Letters to Malcolm*, we normally began our meeting with some bible-study according to a pre-arranged plan. We might take several weeks over a book of the bible, though we sometimes chose passages on a particular theme. A priest or a lay person with some biblical training would speak to us briefly about the original setting and aim of the passage as far as it could be known. Our own experience can naturally help us to understand the experience behind scriptural passages; but we were rather on guard against saying subjectively: 'This is what the passage says to me,' without this first more objective study. For it is sometimes easy for us to say just how a passage seems to fit in with our own experience, and then to go on to claim for our personal opinions some kind of 'biblical authority'. This danger is also less when a number of people discuss a passage together from different angles. Sometimes we found that we couldn't come to an agreement about the original meaning of the passage or about the light it threw on our lives together. Our agreement to differ had then to be the report of our exploration to date. Even so they very often used to be exhilarating meetings; and time usually went too fast.

Before long the chairman would ask us to keep at least five minutes of silence. Then if we wished we could make brief reflections which were sometimes like meditation. These often led on to spontaneous thanksgivings and petition. Occasionally someone might wish to make an apology and ask for forgiveness. Praise was prominent. But sometimes we had a kind of 'Quaker silence', or were drawn to a kind of shared adoration, again without words.

Towards the end of our evening the chairman would gather together our praying in a collect or in some spontaneous prayer of his own. We used to spend the last five or ten minutes in conversation, seeing what we should do in preparation for our next meeting, and— quite important—seeing if there was any service to others which individually or together we should try to do before then.

In recent years many of these groups have been influenced by the charismatic movement, which I have experienced in various forms in the States, in Africa, in South-East Asia and in Australasia, as well as here in England. The renewal it has brought is clear. It is quite beyond me to try to evaluate it. My hope is that it will leaven the whole Church. The leaven in the parable lost itself in the loaf it leavened. I hope this movement will lose itself in the Church, as it renews the Church. Perhaps we can see a parallel in the liturgical movement; that movement first had to have a separate existence to point to the need for renewal, but now it has been able largely to merge itself in the general life of the Church.

I could not at this moment write a book on prayer without looking at the charismatic movement's particular influence on the life of prayer. It has brought a deeper desire for God, a sincerity, a spontaneity and a joy into the total prayers of many people. But what about 'praying in tongues'? This in my own opinion – and I speak as a friend—is a subsidiary element in the charismatic movement. It is there in the New Testament church, though not so widespread as some of my charismatic friends imply. Paul placed it among the gifts of the Spirit, but not high among them. Paul spoke in tongues, although Jesus did not.

In a *koinonia* meeting people may find themselves speaking with tongues, particularly, perhaps, when we express our praise. Our praise, our joy may sometimes be so deep that we cannot find words to express it or, as some might say, they run out of words. I myself then find it quite natural to be silently joyful before God. And that kind of silence is for me and for many people more expressive than any words. But at this point some friends of mine have told me that they 'let go' and find that they are speaking with tongues. Often it is quiet, *sotto voce*. The speaker usually has a sense of release and also of the presence of God. It often leads to a deep love of God and a greater sensitivity and love towards others. I can well understand the release and the real relief that this experience might bring to people frustrated by their own slowness of speech both in praying and in ordinary life.

But there is a danger here, for it may be difficult for

some of those who speak with tongues not to feel more richly gifted by the Spirit than those who do not; and the latter, not to feel 'left out' and inferior—or even guilty. And at times the charismatic groups step up pressure to try to induce this 'gift' in others. I have seen this myself in Africa. And these methods have produced ill feelings and sometimes divisions among Christians. We need always to remember Paul's words: 'I may speak in tongues of men and of angels, but if I am without love, I am a sounding gong or a clanging cymbal'; and again we should seek the Giver more than his gifts. The question still remains—how can we, alone and together, best express with thankful hearts our praise and adoration of God? Yet these *koinonia* and similar groups are concerned not only with praying but also with love in daily life and with care for all our neighbours.

Fraternity Groups

I have shared the life of people who lived close to one another in college or hostel, in extended family group or Christian commune. These very different groups I have put together under the title 'fraternity groups'. I stayed in one in New Zealand, and we had long discussions on how best to plan for our communal prayer. The core of this group lived together in a largish house; the rest, some married couples and some single people, lived in their own homes or flats nearby. We realised that we must remain free for what the Spirit would make clear for us in the future. But our provisional plan was for as many as possible to come together for prayer twice a day; one of these times should be chiefly for what I called 'shared receptive praying', with a fair amount of silence; and the other should be corporate 'giving-prayer' with thanksgiving and intercession. The second of these times we agreed should have a simple planned liturgical shape. Previously members had taken turns to lead this second time of prayer as they wished, but I gather it hadn't worked very well; it had been rather hit-and-miss. For *regular* corporate prayer it seems to me you need a fairly fixed outline of worship, with variety and freedom in details. In particular I think such worship requires a carefully-planned lectionary, a sort of home-base for all our other uses of the bible.

When members of the group could not come to our worship together, we recommended them at the very least to read privately the daily passage from the lectionary; and to regard this not as a burden, a chore, but as a desired link with their partners in our corporate life of prayer.

Prayer with Friends

Besides these varied prayer-groups, perhaps we should more often pray spontaneously in unplanned moments with friends. When we share some good news or face some problem, why shouldn't we pray together? Naturally our attention should be focused on God, however conscious we may be of our friends. We must never pray as a candid friend of mine said a little too satirically of someone who prayed with him: 'He prayed a prayer for me loaded with advice.' Prayers obliquely aimed at a friend are as unauthentic as prayers aimed at fellow-members of a group. When we pray, we pray to God.

Yet when friends pray together, they are drawn both nearer to God and also nearer to one another by the Spirit. If we are just starting to pray together, we might begin with short spontaneous prayers in place of the conventional graces which we used to say at meal times. To use a hymn or a psalm might help to accustom us to praying together. As our shyness wears off, we could move towards a more personal kind of prayer. I remember praying for the first time with a businessman, a friend of mine for years. After reading together a few verses from a letter of Paul and then some minutes of silence, we prayed aloud together about each other's work and responsibilities. It meant a good deal to me, and perhaps even more when a day or two later I received a letter from him, saying how much it had helped him and had deepened our friendship. Looking back over the years, I recall other rather longer times of prayer with friends, spent mostly in silence, but also with spontaneous and quite unselfconscious words. We had a shared awareness of God, and jointly perhaps we were in a way exploring his love. We might be more alert, more ready for these times. They may appear to be small things, but possibly they are a foretaste of that shared contemplative experience of prayer of St Augustine and his mother Monica. He tells us of it in his *Confessions*. It happened not long before her death, at the port of Ostia, from which they were expecting to sail. 'She and I stood alone by a window, which looked over a garden within the house where we were staying. There we talked together, she and I alone, in deep joy. We were seeking together in the presence of that truth, which Thou art. While we were talking of and longing for Thy wisdom, we did with all the effort of our heart for an instant attain to it. Then sighing and leaving there the first fruits of our spirit, we returned to the sound of our own voices.'

10

WORSHIP

*Worship together may take us a good deal
further than we should have gone alone.*

T. R. GLOVER

THERE is a springtime blossoming of small informal
groups that meet for prayer and worship, like those we
discussed in the last chapter. They are one of the signs
of a renewed Christian vitality. I come upon them
widely in my travels. On the other hand I see in many
places—with remarkable exceptions—a decline in num-
bers at the normal church services. With sharply rising
financial costs, we shall not be able to maintain all our
church buildings. Congregations of different churches
will have to learn to share one church building. This
may have at least one good result, that is, of leading us,
not rashly, but thoughtfully, towards Christian unity.
There is also at the moment a disparagement of large
church services—and not least by some enthusiastic
members of these small groups; they claim that church
services are too often cold and formalistic.

Reasons for Worship

But personally I have become convinced that we need
church services as well as small groups—and this for
two reasons.

First, because Christian worship has in its fundamental intention the desire to unite together men and women of all kinds. 'There is no such thing,' Paul said, 'as Jew and Greek, slave and freeman, male and female; for you are all one person in Christ Jesus.' Our gathering together for worship is intended to point and to lead towards God's ultimate purpose—'to be put into effect when the time is ripe: namely, that the universe, all in heaven and on earth, might be brought into a unity in Christ'. Small groups may be springs of new life to vitalise the whole Christian community. But they are very often groups of the like-minded. If they are not to become just coteries, their members need to meet with men and women of different backgrounds both in worship as well as in life.

The forms of worship in our churches, because they must try to meet the needs and temperaments of a wider range of people, will have to be of a different style from the intimate prayers of small house-groups. We must all be prepared for this because, diverse as we are, we are yet all members of one another in the Lord. This does not mean that our church worship need be drab or monotonous—a kind of lowest-common-denominator worship, which will neither offend nor revitalise anybody. Colour, song and joy are often needed.

For another reason too, the forms of worship should be something wider and deeper than we could have devised for ourselves in our small groups. The corporate worship of the Church expresses not only the faith as we have so far grasped it, but the faith, so much greater than ourselves, which has begun to grasp us. One of the rôles of worship in church is to draw us towards a depth of prayer and towards an understanding of God beyond what we have as yet reached. *In the Church's worship we do not only express ourselves, but are being drawn beyond ourselves*. 'Worship', wrote Evelyn Underhill, 'is in its deepest sense creative and redemptive. Only in so far as this adoring acknowledgement of Reality more and more penetrates his life does man himself become real.'

Secondly, there is a need, at least in towns and cities, for church services of considerable size, where enquirers can come and go without being pressed to do anything. There have been times in my own life, as I have mentioned before, when I just wanted to come and go. At a certain stage some seekers rightly wish to be anonymous. If they are left alone as long as they wish to be left alone, they may later be very grateful for some kind of small informal group.

Attempts are being made over a large part of Christendom, probably more vigorously than ever before, to improve our forms of worship—to give them a clearer structure, to make them easier to follow, to make them easily intelligible and to help congregations to participate in them more. In fact these changes may in some places have gone so far as to reduce too much the essential sense of mystery in worship.

Involvement in Worship

But clearly more needs to be done. How fatally easy it is for regular churchgoers to let their worship become routine and superficial. Perhaps I could suggest four things to help to avoid this danger.

First, we need to give some thought to *preparing* for worship. Where the church publishes its lectionary of readings, it is very useful to read one or more of these passages a day or two beforehand. In preparation for the main Sunday service we should examine our lives and repent of our faults, especially if it is the holy communion. In our recent welcome stress on the joy of worship and its corporate nature, some of us may easily lose, I think, this other side and become rather superficial. Our true joy is joy through the cross.

When it is possible, five minutes in silence at church before a service may make a great deal of difference to it. We should pray for those who are going to lead the service, for our fellow-worshippers, for ourselves. But we must not pack too much into these moments: we should rather quieten ourselves and, as in our other times of 'settling down' for prayer, remember that this God, who is love, enfolds us like the air we breathe; and now we are coming together to praise him, to open our hearts to him. Much of our worship is spoilt before it begins—for lack of such preparation; at least that is my impression.

Secondly, we are called to *participate* as thoroughly as we can. At home we have begun to get ourselves ready for this. Now we have come to join in a concerted action—'that together you may with one voice glorify the Father of our Lord Jesus Christ.' Sometimes listening to a choir motet we can indeed be drawn to God. But in general we should really join in the worship— not of course with that artificial and often selfconscious heartiness which can so easily put others off. But we should say and sing, not mumble and hum.

Thirdly, we come to *receive*. We receive encouragement from the spirit of the worship and of the congregation. We come to listen to scripture, not to find unrealistic simple answers to our questions, but to receive the impact of the love of God, particularly through the story of the Hebrew people, and above all through Jesus Christ, a disclosure which has gone on reverberating down the centuries ever since. We come to hear its implications spelt out for our own lives today. There is sometimes chaff to blow off, but the wheat is there, our daily bread.

Fourthly, we come in *gratitude* to offer—to God—our prayers, our hymns, our attention, our hearts. 'Come, and let yourselves be built, as living stones, into a spiritual temple: become a holy priesthood, to offer spiritual sacrifices acceptable to God through Jesus Christ.' We cannot do this alone, but only through union with Christ and his self-offering. And as we shall see in a later chapter, this shows itself in our daily lives, as we let God use us in his transformation of the world. It is not that work matters supremely and worship helps it, but rather, as William Temple said: 'Worship matters supremely and life tests it.'

EUCHARIST

It is not the feast which draws men nearer, but sincerity.

JOHN CHRYSOSTOM

PRAYING alone, prayer-groups, church services—for many people all these find their focus in the eucharist, the Lord's supper, holy communion, mass or whatever name you know it by. A friend of mine told me how the eucharist became the heart not only of his praying but of his long life of caring for others. He spoke about the occasion when the eucharist first gripped him: 'I still remember,' he said, 'as a student soon after my conversion, early on a dark, foggy, weekday morning at a church in the east-end of London; a eucharist with about a dozen people present—and after my communion I felt as if I was walking on air.' He mentioned other moving experiences, and they seemed to come when he was most involved in caring for underprivileged people. He has spent thirty years working among Africans. He was there in the years of *Uhuru*, the call to freedom, when country after country claimed and with such high hopes celebrated its self-government. He has worked hard with Africans during all their exhilarations and dashed hopes. He says he could not have gone on through it all without the supernatural strength and love that came to him almost daily through the eucharist. He, like the rest of us, did not always have deep feelings at the time of the eucharist, but he knew he had to go on and on whether he felt 'emotionally dead or just very tired'. He has grown certain that the eucharist is always an open door through which the Lord comes into our hearts and lives; and the greater his concern for his neighbours, the more he found in the eucharist. This is what I have found too.

The Eucharist down the Ages

The eucharist has come to mean so much to me and my friend—not merely on personal, temperamental grounds. For Jesus himself, it seems, made the eucharist central for us when he said: 'Do this in remembrance of me.' And at what a solemn moment he asked us to do this—the night before Good Friday, the very eve of his laying down his life on the cross for love of us. His request comes to us from the culminating point of his life of unceasing love. So the basic reason why we share in the eucharist is love, our love responding to his love and to his request that night.

From the beginning we can watch the Christians coming together to 'do this' in remembrance of him; Paul, for instance, breaks his journey at Troas to 'do this' on the first day of the week. In the second century Justin Martyr tells us that all Christians come together for the eucharist every Lord's day because Jesus rose that day. The eucharist makes every Sunday an Easter.

So it went on all over the Christian church for fifteen hundred years; and it has gone on unbroken among the Roman Catholics and Orthodox until today. In the course of the centuries distortions had crept into the eucharist. So at the Reformation the question arose whether the eucharist was the best pattern for worship

144

every Sunday. Even then the great reformers, Luther and Calvin, wished it to go on week by week. But they could not carry their followers with them, the re-actions against the medieval distortions were so strong. However, in recent years the weekly eucharist has been more and more re-established among Anglicans and to a less extent amongst Protestants.

These changes have come through the liturgical movement. For many years I knew it while it was quite unofficial. The first of the revised forms of the eucharist I celebrated—and how thrilled I was!—was during my visit to the united Church of South India in 1963. The Church of England had its first thoroughly revised liturgy in 1967, and the Roman Catholic church in 1971. This movement has now spread in one form or another to very many churches.

The results have been predominantly good. Many more Christians have come to see the centrality of the eucharist. It has given them a service easier to follow; for they see it has a clear structure, a double feasting on the Word of God and on the Bread of Life. The worship of the church has been brought nearer to life as it is today. It has given members of the congrega-tion a more active part in the service, and also a stronger sense of fellowship with one another. We have so much to be thankful for; and I should like to help you to enter more deeply into this form of worship.

The Wonder of the Eucharist

There is a danger that we may for several reasons lose our sense of wonder at the eucharist. I will mention two. First, in recent revisions there have been so many and so frequent changes in the wording that we may have become too preoccupied with the words and are in danger of losing the sense of wonder in the eucharist which lies behind the words and deeper than even the best-chosen words. Secondly, there have been attempts to press for one standardised form for this service—a 'parish communion', as it is called among Anglicans. But we really need a great variety of ways to express the many-sided mystery of the eucharist. It is so much more than words and forms.

The eucharist is essentially God's immense, unchanging love in Christ coming to us, our responding in love, our offering ourselves through Christ to be transformed by love and so being set free to share this love in the world. This needs to be celebrated, like human friendship and love, in ways beyond counting. The eucharist with its many facets sparkles like a diamond. It is by being united to Christ in love that we become more united to one another in the Body of Christ throughout the world. Partaking of the eucharistic body of Christ, we become the worldwide Body of Christ.

Before each eucharist we could perhaps all kneel in silence and reflect in our different ways on the wonder of this feast which spans space and time. I'm a lucky man. I can see again the eucharist in many places to which my work has taken me. I recall a colourful eucharist in our Anglican cathedral in the Fiji Islands, where understandably there are tensions between the Fijis, who have the land rights, the immigrant Indian labourers, some of whom are now rich, the Chinese shopkeepers, the Americans and English. But what a joy it was that morning—the first Sunday after Easter. We all sang together with organ, drums and guitars. We even sang in Fiji, Hindi and English, for the service and hymns were typed out phonetically in normal script. It was all the easier because everything was well sprinkled with alleluias. In my short broadcast address I tried to use their gospel for the day to help us all truly to feed together; first, the hearts of the two men on the road to Emmaus burned within them when the Risen Jesus explained the scriptures; and then, he was 'known to them in the breaking of the bread'. And so with us now. We, different as we were, were being tangibly made one by this glorious feasting on the Word of God and the Bread of Life.

Or my thoughts and prayers go back to one of the few churches still open in Moscow, packed with people. There I stood with them, shoulder to shoulder, for three hours, praising God in their well-loved liturgy. What faith, what joy, even after all those years of anti-religious propaganda! God makes us in the eucharist really and firmly the Body of Christ.

And I remember a Sunday morning beside the Lake of Galilee, so still, just after a golden dawn. There I celebrated the eucharist with a flat boulder as an altar and the waves lapping at our feet. How often the Lord had been there! How truly he is here to strengthen us and make us one!

Or my memory carries me back to my study in a seminary where I taught in New York. One evening we were there packed together. We had been discussing what Paul wrote to the Philippians about our being of one heart and mind; a unity, the apostle said, springing out of our life in Jesus, the Son of God who, for love of us, made himself one with us and died on the cross for us. How exactly right it felt to go on to share together in the one bread and the one cup of Christ!

And I see how this wonderful eucharist runs through our lives like a thread of gold. I well remember the wedding of two student friends of mine on a warm sunny day in a village church in Sussex with the scent of new-mown hay drifting in through the wide-open doors, and how I celebrated the nuptial eucharist there for them. Or again I think of the nun in whose small cell I said a simple eucharist, as she lay dying; her Sisters were singing the twenty-third psalm, *Le Seigneur est mon berger*; and in a few hours she herself was with the Lord she loved after her long life of praying and service sustained by this feast.

We must never let our eucharist become mere routine. We must preserve in it a sense of wonder. And, there, we are close to *all* who are in Christ.

Structure of the Eucharist

The revised services inspired by the liturgical movement, with their clear, twofold structure, remind us of what Thomas à Kempis long ago taught us: 'I need to be fed from two tables—the table of the holy word and the table of the holy bread.' We come hungry—more than we realise—hungry for God's love, just as we hunger for human companionship and love. If we had fewer words and more silence in the eucharist, we might be better fed.

To have some quiet time at home or, better, to be quiet together in church is, where practicable, an excellent 'way in' to the eucharist. Young and old can be helped to enter into this quietness more readily than we sometimes think. And when we have silence, let us not fill it up with a plethora of words in our minds, but rather let us look contemplatively, receptively to God himself, whose love and generosity embrace all. The Giver can give only if we are open to receive.

Here at the beginning—or in some liturgies a little later—we confess our own failings. We learn how to do this trustfully but not vaguely; we ask God's forgiveness for all men; and we receive forgiveness.

The heart of the first part of the eucharist is *feasting on the scriptures*. It matters much what is read; it matters even more *how* we receive it. Listening to the bible at the eucharist is more like going to a concert than to a classroom or lecture-hall. We speak of a fine concert as a feast of music; we are inwardly enriched by it. So at the eucharist we are enriched, we are fed, by the bible. We need to remind ourselves that the bible is the record of how God has step by step disclosed and conveyed his love to his people, our spiritual ancestors. We feel ourselves called with Abraham and the prophets by God's love. We know ourselves disciplined and purified by God's love when we see his people in exile. We see them restored to be 'a light to all peoples, a beacon for the nations'. They do not rise to their responsibility and opportunities. And we ask ourselves whether we are now rising to ours. Then in the gospels we see Christ in his ceaseless love taking on himself this responsibility of light-bearing. But rejected by his people, deserted by his disciples, he goes to the cross, unswervingly loyal to God's love. He dies, he is restored to life, he sends his Spirit to his new people. In the epistles we see how they begin to understand and to carry his love to all men.

We watch all this not as remote history, but as something pressing upon us today and never more so—as we shall soon see—than in the eucharist. So as we listen, we marvel at God's love, we respond afresh to his call in our responsibilities, we repent of our lack of courage, we give ourselves afresh, strengthened by the Spirit of the Lord. We need time to do this—a few minutes of silence after the readings or perhaps during some psalm or hymn chosen to prolong our reflection. As a parish priest I have known the responsibility, the joy and the difficulty of helping people through the sermon really to feast on these scriptures. Our reading the bible at home is an invaluable preparation for feasting on it in church.

About this point in the service comes appropriately the intercession. We come to God bringing in our hearts those we love and those for whom we have responsibility. And intercession, as we have seen, involves giving ourselves to God in love, so that he can use us in the service of those we pray for. Many of the revised services suggest a little silence again here, so that our personal prayers can be tributaries into the one Church's great river of intercession flowing to God.

Then we come to the *feasting on the Bread of Life.* Our revised services show that this means simply the four actions which Jesus did at the last supper. He took the bread and wine, he blessed God, he broke the bread, he gave the bread and wine over which thanks had been given. These are things done more than things said. Jesus said, '*Do* this'. We smother eloquent actions with words.

First, *we place bread and wine* on the altar-table. Our worship is our love, responding to his love. Our love places in Love's hand all our daily life—the bread as the symbol of toil and difficulty, and the sparkling wine of our joys and affections. 'There are you,' St Augustine said, 'on the altar'; though we can only give, because Jesus by loving us as far as his death is freeing us from possessiveness.

Secondly, we bless, *we thank God.* This is our duty and our joy. We do this not alone but with Christians across the world—oceans separate, the eucharist unites

—and with loved ones the other side of the stream of death. We are freed from our narrowness and loneliness. So in our name God is thanked for creation, for Christ's coming, living, dying and rising, for the Spirit and the Church. Our Amen makes this thanksgiving our own, an Amen which Jerome said in his day used 'to reverberate like heavenly thunder'.

The words translated 'Do this in remembrance of me' almost certainly do not mean 'Remember the Christ of past history'; but rather, 'When you do this, then his living, dying and rising are through the Spirit brought into us at the present moment with all their power'; and also we have a foretaste, a pre-experience, of Christ's ultimate gathering of all into himself. Dr C. H. Dodd wrote: 'Past, present and future are indissolubly united in the sacrament.' Human friendship and love helps us to grasp this; for memories of shared experience can come back to us as more than *mere* memories; and eagerly awaited meetings can give us already a pre-experience of the joys to come.

We may not know *how* this happens, but it is for us nothing vague, still less doubtful. As the handshake is to friendship, as the embrace is to love, so is eating and drinking the eucharistic bread and wine to our real encounter with Christ. The tangible conveys the intangible, an intangible deeply real.

Yet I remember how often people have told me of their disappointment that they have so little feeling of Christ's presence at holy communion. This might be our fault; as barriers can build up between friends, so can they between the Lord and ourselves. But this lack of feeling comes often from no fault of ours. In loyal human love feelings fall and rise. God's love is often too profound to be felt. The depth of our communion with the Lord—either at the eucharist or anywhere else—is not tested by the vividness of our feelings. We know its reality, not through our feelings, but through the Lord's promise to be with us. And Jesus does not come to give us deep feelings, but to unite us to himself in order to bring his loving service to the world. His love involved the cross. Through the eucharist we let our offering of ourselves be drawn into his sacrifice of love. 'He has willed,' said St Augustine, 'that *we* also should be his sacrifice.'

Thirdly, *the bread is broken*, ready to be shared by all. This receiving of the Lord in love and our responding in love sacrificial and joyful, happens to us one by one, yet not alone, but together as the one body of Christ. 'When we break the bread, is it not a sharing in the body of Christ? Because there is one loaf, we, many as we are, are one body; for it is one loaf of which we all partake.'

Fourthly, we *receive* the eucharistic bread and wine together. This is as personal as the Risen Jesus meeting Mary Magdalene at Easter dawn. As we meet him, we meet one another in him. We are one in him. We need silence enough to contemplate his love immediately after receiving holy communion or after the service and perhaps again later in the day.

Our Preparation for the Eucharist

How grateful we are for the liturgical movement. But it has not, as I and thousands of others had hoped, led to a rebirth of the Church for its service in the world. The liturgical movement needs to be married to the renewal of contemplation. The Lord can give and give, but unless our hearts are opened through contemplation to receive and to share, what can happen?

How can our own prayers, daily receiving- and giving-prayers, flow into and 'personalise' our eucharist? We each need to be continually on the alert to discover *our own ways* to do this. This is not asking for more of our time for prayer. It requires only the love-inspired alertness which will reshape and redirect our normal prayers on the day before our communion.

Paul himself wrote: 'A man must test himself before eating his share of the bread and drinking from the cup.' We are not required to be faultless, but to repent, to be forgiven, to be prepared for this renewed coming of the Lord into our lives. It is like the way we prepare a room for a guest: we put some flowers there and select a few books for the bed-table—small things, but sacramental signs of welcome and love.

I can only tell you what I do, or try to do. You may find for yourself something more meaningful. First, I carry over one or two specific thanksgivings from my daily prayer to incorporate into the eucharist so that it is rooted into the realness of life as I experience it. Secondly, I am a little extra thorough in my evening self-examination; then there is something to give definiteness and reality to my confession and forgiveness in the eucharist. Besides the confession we make together in the eucharist, some of us find it a great help from time to time, such as Christmas and Easter, to make our confession individually and to receive God's absolution through a priest or minister. This is one of the ways a guide can be very useful indeed. Bonhoeffer used to recommend this practice. Thirdly, in preparation for the eucharist I select from my daily prayers a few particular intercessions to weave into the Church's prayers. Personally, as I have said, I have to begin my ordinary prayer with what is near to me and let it spread out to wider concerns, or else my praying remains very shallow. Fourthly, I also go to the eucharist with some particular request for myself, perhaps about some task I have on hand. Fifthly, if I can find time, I try to spend some minutes in quiet meditative praying on the epistle or gospel for the day or on a eucharistic hymn, or else on a eucharistic passage from the scriptures or from other books. This helps me to approach the eucharist with faith, to make the best use of its moments of silence, and to prepare me to return to share in the world the divine love I shall have received.

The Eucharist and Life

Thomas Merton used to say that for him the best time in the whole day for thanksgiving and prayer was the time in church after holy communion. And you would agree, I expect, that we should continue this thanksgiving in our prayer at home. But real gratitude means not only the prayers of our lips; it also shows itself in the quality of our lives. The letter to the Ephesians—and one of our Anglican communion prayers—speaks of expressing our thankfulness by doing those good works which God has prepared for us to walk in. So each communion, besides deepening both our union with God and also our love for one another, should lead us to do something specific in gratitude—a job to be finished off at once, a letter to be written and posted, a person to be encouraged that day, an effort to get something done where justice demands it. Prayer that finds its focus in the eucharist is contemplative but also constructive.

To strengthen our life of prayer and our service in the world some of us may be able to go to the eucharist more often, perhaps on weekdays. This is indeed a privilege. Soon after his death someone spoke of the place the eucharist had held in the life of a priest, who had had a great influence on me. His life had been packed full with his work, constantly interrupted by the chores of administration, which he would never allow to be called chores. Then at night when interruptions were over, he would turn to his ceaseless correspondence and give time to prayer. So his work went on and on, year after year. Luckily he had a sense of humour and the constitution of a horse. He was tough on himself, but gentle with others. And he used to teach that 'we give ourselves to God in every sacrament, in every prayer', and that 'we live the rest of our lives in order to carry out the sacrifice, this gift of ourselves to God, to completeness'. And it was said of him: 'All the details of every day came into his self-sacrifice, united with the eucharist that he offered at the altar every morning.'

What a wonder the eucharist is in all its variety, sparkling like a diamond! Yet it is always and everywhere the same. For it is the feast spread before us by the love of God, a feast both on his Word and on the Bread of Life.

But his great love cannot feed us, unless it meets sincerity in us. So perhaps we should now quietly consider our own sincerity—sincerity in our preparing, and sincerity in our responding, which means trying to carry his love, strength and joy to our families and friends, to our work and responsibilities in the world. 'We love, because he loved us first.'

CONTEMPLATION AND THE WORLD

For contemplation he and valour formed.

JOHN MILTON

'DEVOTION is neither private nor public prayer,' so in his characteristically downright language William Law began his book, *A Serious Call*, which incidentally influenced John Wesley deeply as a young man. Then William Law went on to say: 'But prayers, whether private or public, are particular parts of devotions. Devotion signifies *a life given, or devoted to God.*'

It might be very useful for us at this point in our journey, don't you think, to pause for a few moments, and think over rather carefully that basic statement about life?

It is a high ideal. We may never reach it—certainly not in our own strength; but we can draw upon God's strength to bring us nearer to it.

But on reflection, isn't that ideal something to keep practically before us—the devotion of our lives, given to God, to be used in realistic ways, for service in his world? It demands courage, but John Milton says that man was made for valour as well as for contemplation.

Deep down we feel, I think, that what matters fundamentally is—not just devotions, but devotion; not just prayers, but life permeated by prayer; not just contemplation, but contemplation and transformation of the world.

To Work is to Pray?

I had better, in passing, guard myself against a possible misunderstanding of what I have just said. For nowadays some people—sincere Christians among them —interpret the old saying *Laborare est orare*, 'to work is to pray', as meaning that working in the right spirit is itself *all* the praying we need do. The nearest I could come to their point of view is to say that working in that spirit should be an integral continuation of our praying—just as the infra-red waves of heat are continuous with the spectrum of light—and this working should be pervaded by the spirit of prayer. Jesus worked like that—*but* he had also his times alone in prayer. And many of us are convinced that we could not work —certainly not work in the spirit of Jesus—unless we receive God's own strength; and to receive this strength we ourselves are convinced that we must set apart times to be alone with God or times with him in company with others.

I agree with those who are most active in service about the enormous needs of our world, the need for struggle, for social and political action. I am haunted too by the words of Mother Teresa: 'The biggest disease today is the feeling of being unwanted, uncared for,' which underlie so many of our problems. Then I remember too what Thomas Merton said: 'Action is the stream, contemplation the spring.'

So my problem—and perhaps yours—is how do we make this 'link up' between prayers and life, between contemplation and action?

Three men, very different from one another—they

now seem to me like friends—have helped me with this problem by their writings and letters: Brother Lawrence by teaching me how to bring my praying into the heart of my living in the world; Jean Pierre de Caussade by showing me how to cope with the insistent demands of contemporary living; and William Temple by making it clear to me that this 'link up' is thoroughly practicable and can be done with joy. Perhaps one or other of these three could help you. Anyway, why not dip into their books and see?

Brother Lawrence

I don't know why I have been so blind. Until recently I have thought the place where my praying must be done is either in church or my room. But if you come to think of it, most of our praying should be done in those places where we spend most hours of our lives. Brother Lawrence is teaching me that. I often now slip into my pocket his little gem of a book, *The Practice of the Presence of God*; it has already travelled thousands of miles with me.

Brother Lawrence was born in Lorraine in 1611. He fought in the Thirty Years' War, was wounded in the leg, and left with a limp for the rest of his life. After his discharge from the army he became a manservant in the household of a government official; he describes himself as 'a great awkward fellow who broke everything'. When he was fifty-five, he was received as a lay brother among the Carmelites in Paris. He died there twenty-five years later, having spent almost the whole time in charge of the kitchen. Life for him was humdrum—as it is for some of us—but he learned a great deal about 'real living'.

He tells us that he was converted at eighteen, about

the time he became a soldier. It happened so simply and so profoundly. He says that he was just taken out of himself by looking at a tree leafless in winter and realising that at springtime the leaves would appear and then the flowers and fruit. This simple contemplation stirred up in him, he says, so deep a love for God that 'he could not tell whether it had increased in above forty years that he had lived since then'. These 'high moments', which have come to Brother Lawrence and to some of us, open our eyes to the reality of the spiritual, give us a glimpse of what is to come, but above all encourage us to *press on* steadily beyond these experiences.

His writings, which come from the end of his life, after he had persevered for many years, have the marks of authenticity and clarity. But he speaks of the difficulties of his early days in the life of prayer, of how he needed 'fidelity in those drynesses, insensibilities and irksomenesses in prayer, by which God tries our love for him'; and of how at those times he even felt it all might be a delusion. Then he goes on to show us how to do what he learned in his own experience—'to school ourselves to find our joy in the divine companionship'.

This brings me to the thing that I myself have most to learn from Brother Lawrence—*to take my praying into the heart of my living in the world*. We each have to discover our own way. It sounds obvious, but I have done so little about it. Brother Lawrence's way is that 'we should *establish* ourselves in a sense of God's presence by *continually conversing with him*'. The idea might seem naïve if it meant telling God of what was going on; instead of meaning, as it does, honestly opening ourselves to him, so that his love can enter and continually transform our daily lives.

This frequent turning to God during the day requires of us a *serious* effort. It means training ourselves, at least to begin with. We can—to take tiny examples—pray for a person as we are taking up our pen to write to him, for a friend as we see him coming towards us, or for our family, as we lay the meal table for them. We can associate the small things we do every day with our normal practices of prayer; as we open a book or newspaper, we can say: 'Thank you also for the scriptures, the good news'; or in the act of sitting down for a meal: 'Thank you, Lord, also for the Bread of Life'; or as we take something to drink: 'Thank you, Lord, as well for the Cup of Salvation'; or as the telephone or door bell rings, we can say the words of St Patrick: 'Christ in mouth of friend or stranger.' Some of us can repeat to ourselves a verse from our meditation frequently during the day. Others can learn the use of the 'Jesus-Prayer', so dear to the Orthodox. All these phrases of prayer, so brief in themselves, should gradually fill the day with what Cassian called 'uninterrupted prayerfulness of mind'.

'I made prayer my business *as much all the day long* as at the appointed times,' Brother Lawrence said. Perhaps it was easier for him than for many of us in our busy world. But it is even more important when we are overpressed and quiet times are hard to find; for then these tiny prayers may have to be almost our only prayers. Our daily walk will become a heavy trudge without them. These small prayers meant so much for Brother Lawrence that he never asked his superior for extra periods of prayer; in fact he said: 'I have quitted all forms of devotion and set prayers except those to which my duty obliges me. And I make it my business only to persevere in God's presence; or, to speak more precisely, in an habitual, silent and secret conversation with God, which often causes me joys inwardly.'

Another part of our self-training will be how we use our odd moments of waiting during the day—waiting for a train or a bus, or a telephone to be free—moments we so easily fill up with restless grumbling—and the grumbling doesn't speed anything up. Brother Lawrence, remembering his years as a soldier, wrote: 'A little lifting up of the heart suffices; a little remembrance of God, one act of inward worship, though upon a march with sword in hand, are prayers which, however short, are nevertheless very acceptable to God.' As we grow in love for God, our thoughts turn naturally to God at these times, like a lover thinking of his beloved.

Brother Lawrence of course still maintained his daily periods of prayer. In his early days as a novice he tells us that he used to *meditate* on the fundamentals of our Christian faith—and this he acknowledges was very useful and laid for him a good foundation for Christian praying and living. But now he says he turns to God at these times in a simpler, more receptive, more *contemplative* way. Looking back over his years of prayer he writes: 'We must know before we can love. In order to know God, we must often think of him, and when we come to love him, we shall then also think of him often, for in our heart will be our treasure.'

Brother Lawrence's ordinary daily work was in this way gladdened—and so it can be for us. 'The time of business,' he says, 'does not with me differ from the time of prayer; and in the noise and clutter of my kitchen, while several persons are at the same time calling for different things, I possess God in as great tranquillity as if I were upon my knees at the sacrament.'

Not that he was always in his busy kitchen, or even in his monastery. He tells how he was sent to Burgundy to buy the provisions of wine for his society, which was a very unwelcome task for him, for he had no mind for business. And because of his lameness he could not go about the boat except by rolling himself over the casks. However, he gave himself no uneasiness about it, nor about the purchase of the wine. He told God that it was *His* business that he was about; and he then found it all worked out very well.

Père de Caussade

I have, as you may have guessed, a busy, well-packed life. And Jean Pierre de Caussade is teaching me a method of taking things one at a time and of not being irritated by them or overwhelmed by them. This method is contained in his remarkable phrase, 'the sacrament of the present moment'. His best-known book, *Abandonment to the Divine Providence*, is now in paperback, though unfortunately without his letters that give the standard edition a much more human touch.

He was born in 1675. As a young Jesuit priest he taught classics, physics and logic. He was never a public figure. He conducted retreats; and for a short time he was in turn the superior of two Jesuit houses—a task he disliked and wrote about with wry humour. He died at the age of seventy-five after bearing years of blindness with uncomplaining fortitude.

Let us look at his arresting phrase, 'the sacrament of the present moment'. Few words have recently helped me more. And there is more in them for me still to discover. Père de Caussade is convinced that, because God's very nature is unchangeable love, God is loving each of us at *every* moment. Therefore it follows, he maintains, that God's love is somehow coming to us through *what is happening now*. God's love cannot directly reach us through yesterday's happenings or tomorrow's, but through what is going on now. Very soon we will consider what this implies about how we cope with the demands of our everyday lives.

Père de Caussade says again and again that God intends his love should reach us not only through the holy sacrament but through every moment of our lives. De Caussade asks: 'Why should not *every moment of our lives be a sort of communion with divine love*?' He does not of course derogate the holy sacrament, but he declares: 'God makes of all things mysteries and sacraments of love.' How then can we receive 'the sacrament of the present moment'? There are two things required.

First, we need to pray to have deeply and constantly rooted in us this conviction that God is love. I have written already of the clouds that so often threaten to obscure this fact from us. But always we must try to see, piercing through those clouds, that ray of divine love seen in the life and passion of our Lord. And we need to receive this love into ourselves, day by day, by faith, confidently committing ourselves to God. About this Père de Caussade wrote: 'Did the Lord not prove that he loved us more than life itself, since he laid down his life for us? And can we not be assured that, having done so much, he will never forget us?'

Therefore God's love can reach *you* just now, as you are reading these words—through this present moment —not through time past, nor through time yet to come, but just through this present moment as it arrives: 'Eternity caught in a span'.

Secondly, we have to train ourselves in how to approach this present moment as it comes to us—the job in hand, the squabble to resolve, the stranger to welcome. We know how we try to approach the moment of sacramental communion, to concentrate on it receptively in faith and love. We do the same when we meet a friend. Then this is how to try to approach every moment. This is what de Caussade advises: 'We must cut off all more distant views, we must confine ourselves to the duty of the *present moment* without thinking of what preceded it or what will follow it'; and again he says: 'The duties of each moment are shadows beneath which the divine action lies concealed.' Of course on particular occasions it is our duty—indeed the duty of that particular moment—to consider the future. But de Caussade counsels us: 'Try not to let apprehension about the future or regret about the past flood over into your present living, and make you miserable.'

If only we could remember and approach each moment, as Père de Caussade recommends, it might well through God's grace transform our lives and all our service in the world.

This concentrating on the present and not worrying about the future or the past requires a lot of practice. Père de Caussade tells us how he himself tried to get out of becoming the superior of a Jesuit house at Perpignan. He grumbled; he complained that he had no aptitude for the job. When he arrived, it was worse than he had anticipated. He hated VIP visits—yet the bishop, steward, King's lieutenant, sheriff, garrison officer all called on him. Yet afterwards—to his own surprise—he could write: 'I remain calm and in peace in the midst of a thousand worries and complications in which I should have expected to be overwhelmed.'

The secret of this way of coping with life is what he calls *abandon*, in the sense that a swimmer might float along abandoning himself to the current of a river, instead of battling against it, swimming counter-stream. He sees an example of abandon in Mary's words to God at the annunciation: 'Behold the handmaid of the Lord, be it unto me according to thy word.' He points out that this *abandon* was not reluctant or narrowing but 'something very glorious', which ran afterwards like a thread of gold through all 'occupations, commonplace or lofty' of her life.

Père de Caussade's counsels on 'the sacrament of the present moment' and on *abandon* are beginning to mean so much to me that I would like to share with you a few other closely related themes of this book. I am jotting down my rather amateur reflections also, because I hope you may soon be reading his book for yourself.

First, God can only bring us these desired blessings and can only 'take possession of a soul in so far as it is empty of all confidence in its own actions'. I agree, though I know how much of this is beyond my own present experience. This divine action will involve our purification from self-seeking, a long and perhaps painful refining.

Secondly, he, like some other writers on the life of prayer, says that this purification will involve accepting 'crosses sent by Providence'. This I cannot personally accept, or perhaps I have as yet misunderstood it. We all know that in daily life and love there are difficulties, problems and pain to be borne; and in the life of prayer too. These things have a way of happening in the kind of world we live in. I would prefer not to say that God directly sends these things, but rather that he permits them to happen and enables us to use them in this necessary purification of our lives. And, if we learn to take them, with the help of his Spirit, they have a way of refining, enriching and deepening, not only our love for one another, but our love for God. Perhaps this difficulty which I have at present with de Caussade is linked with his claim to detect the will of God with a clarity which I honestly find impossible.

Thirdly, I have another difficulty with some other words of his: 'We must kill our senses and be stripped of them; their destruction means the reign of faith.' If he means only that special kind of inner silence *during* contemplative praying—and there is a quotation in chapter 8 about this from *The Cloud of Unknowing*— I quite agree; in fact I begin to know how vital this is. But if he means 'this killing of the senses' to cover the whole of life, then it is beyond my understanding; and, further, I do not see it in the life of Jesus and in his endless caring for others.

Fourthly, I must say that in general I find Père de Caussade very encouraging. He is humane. There is no hardness or aloofness in his own writing, particularly in his letters. 'Little falls,' he says, 'are permitted in order to help us to practise humility and patience and to endure ourselves. Our falls, seen in this way, will be far more useful to us than victories that are spoiled by vain complacency.' He says that his method is 'accessible to everybody' and that fundamentally it adds up to doing with *true love* the ordinary things our life demands of us.

William Temple

In spirit William Temple was close to Brother Lawrence and Jean Pierre de Caussade, but in the events of his life very different. What the life of William Temple does for me is to convince me that this 'link up' between devotion and devotions, between life and contemplation, is practicable—and can be done with joy. He was a man of action because he was a man of prayer.

He had, as everyone knows, a dazzling academic career. He lived in a world perhaps less complex than ours. He was so gifted. And some people say life was made too easy for him. But he never lacked courage to speak out, even if what he said might jeopardise his future. His ordination was delayed; doubts caused difficulties. He became—I think a little surprisingly—headmaster of Repton. He moved on to become a leader in church reform, then bishop, and for a couple of years at the end of the war Archbishop of Canterbury. He always had a tightly packed life with an enormous range of interests. He was, for instance, president of the Workers' Education Association for eighteen years before the doors of higher education had been opened wide.

Yet he had an eye for everyone. A small example of this: he was in the chair at a meeting to which I had been invited; I was silent, overawed, for all the others were far senior to me; and then with his discerning smile he turned to me and asked: 'And how does all this strike you? You come to it fresh'; and he treated my stumbling words far more seriously than they deserved.

He was an inspired teacher. He packed the university church at Oxford in the early 30s for a week's course on *Christian Faith and Life*. Religion was then at a low ebb in the university, hardly intellectually respectable. His achievement was to 'put Christianity right back on the map'. The published addresses went through seventeen reprints in twenty years. In the ecumenical movement he was one of the main architects of the World Council of Churches. He was invited to speak to the bankers on 'Finance, Production and Consumption', and to the Institute of Industrial Management on 'The Spirit of Management'. He probably did more than any other churchman to create the atmosphere necessary for setting up the Welfare State in this country.

Although he was so able, you felt he was close to ordinary people like ourselves. When you read his books, you feel he is talking to you. When you met him, he was so human, so accessible, so unruffled—in spite of the incessant demands made on him—and so hilarious. His wife said that they married not because they shared the same interests, but because they laughed at the same things. And there is an apocryphal story about his going to Repton. There was a master there, we will call him A; this man had a gigantic laugh; and Temple said he went to Repton because he was determined 'to outlaugh A on his own ground'. These qualities were not only part of Temple's natural temperament; they were seen to be supernatural also, the fruits of the Spirit within him—love, peace and joy.

In particular we must notice that all this leadership sprang out of his life of prayer, a leadership both unremitting and sensitive. In the packed cathedral when he was made Bishop of Manchester he said: 'Pray for me, I ask you, not chiefly that I may be wise and strong, or any such thing, though for these things I need your prayers. But pray for me chiefly that I may never let go the unseen hand of the Lord Jesus and may live in daily fellowship with him. It is thus that you will most of all help me to help you. And so we shall go forward together.'

He certainly stressed the need of prayer. 'Life and prayer,' he said in the university church at Oxford, 'should be as closely as possible intertwined. God is the ultimate Reality who sustains all existence, including our own lives. To be in actual and living union with him is the fundamental business of life; and everything else follows from that.' So we are not surprised to find him writing to a friend who had recently been made principal of a theological college: 'You will use this as a basis for what we need more than all else—to teach the clergy to be teachers of prayer.'

I have a strong impression that William Temple's praying was very much along the lines of Brother Lawrence's *Practice of the Presence of God*; but he adds to it a qualification without which we might misunderstand Brother Lawrence himself. William Temple says that we should give our entire attention to exacting tasks we have to do—and not to try to think of God then—or we shall not do our best work. We should, he adds, start on those tasks refreshed by the thought of God's love; and when the exertion is over, our minds should return to God. But he emphasises that it is in this sense we should constantly be remembering the presence of God.

In some lectures at Harvard William Temple spoke of worship—almost in our sense of contemplation— and said: 'It is the opening of the heart to receive the love of God; it is the declaration of our need to be fulfilled by him; it is the subjection of our desire to be controlled by him; and as a result of all these together, it is the surrender of our will to be used by him.' He added that, just because our responsibilities in the world require of us such concentration of thought and attention, we cannot perform our ordinary work as duty to God, unless we are also giving times—and abundant times—in which we bring our minds back to the *contemplation* of him.

Finally, William Temple insists that prayer is not preoccupation with our own interests; and he says: 'Bring the needs of the world and the problems of life before God; then leave them with him and wait for a while *in silence not only from speech, but as far as possible from thought*. There is no limit to what God will do by means of us, if we train ourselves to trust him enough.'

Envoy

We set out on this journey together, wishing to discover more about contemplation and prayer in our modern world. We saw that they are both rooted deep in our nature as men and women—our need to 'perceive receptively' and our desire to give ourselves in love and prayer. We live in this twofold rhythm our hearts demand—receiving and giving. We realise more clearly than some of our predecessors that the mystery we wish to explore is beyond words and images. We are not alone on this search; and more than ever before we are a motley crowd. We have trodden together some well-worn tracks. In wooded country we have noticed side paths, not much used yet, but perhaps leading to sunlit glades. Sometimes we have looked into still pools of water, reflecting the sky. We have on our way talked to several experienced guides. We can see some steep climbs ahead. We are already beginning to enter into a land of infinite distances.

On our journey from time to time we have stopped to consider various possibilities in this life of contemplation and prayer. Would it be useful for us now to reflect to see if any overall pattern is emerging, which is practicable?

But to make plans is not to have arrived at the journey's end. Perhaps some of us have before now drawn up plans, and often our good intentions have evaporated. This is how life is. But love only remains love if it loves afresh. So whatever happens, let's try for the future not to give in to discouragement. We can't help, because we are human, the feelings of discouragement eddying around us, but in the power of the Spirit we can stand firm and not let ourselves be carried away by them. A bishop I used to work with—as wise as a twentieth-century Francis de Sales—used to say with excusable exaggeration: 'Discouragement is worse than all faults'—because it opens the door wide to so many of them. Isn't it so? 'And it's worth dropping almost any other work,' the bishop used to add, 'to rescue someone from discouragement.'

The main reason why my own good intentions in the past have often died away has been, I must frankly confess, my self-reliance. I have thought that with a bit more planning and organising I could get it all done myself. But what we cannot do alone, we can do in the company of others. And what we cannot do, the Spirit can. Now is the Spirit's springtime.

As we come to the end of this sketch of our journey, I wonder what you are thinking. My thoughts are turning to my friends, to men and women who in all sorts of places have talked with me about contemplation and prayer, and also to those who may read these pages. I wish them well. I pray for them. I would put my desires for you all into a paraphrase of a prayer, much loved by me, at the end of the third chapter of Paul's letter to the Ephesians:

May we be strengthened by your Spirit in the depths
    of our being.
May Christ live in our hearts through faith.
With love's deep roots and firm foundations,
    may we, in company with each other, discover
    the breadth, the length, the height and depth of
    Christ's love,
    a love beyond all words, beyond all we can ever
    understand.
May our lives in the world be enriched with his love.
We are confident you will do more than we could
    ask or think,
        through the Spirit of Jesus Christ.
        Father of all, Lord of all,
        Abba, Father.

For Further Reading

Abhishiktananda (Henri Le Saux), *Prayer*, SPCK: 1972

Metropolitan Anthony, *Meditations on a Theme*, Mowbrays: 1972

Dietrich Bonhoeffer, *Life Together*, SCM Press: 1965

Alan Ecclestone, *Yes to God*, Darton, Longman & Todd: 1975

Monica Furlong, *Contemplating Now*, Hodder & Stoughton: 1971

André Louf, *Teach us to Pray*, Darton, Longman & Todd: 1974

John Macquarrie, *Paths in Spirituality*, SCM Press: 1972

Thomas Merton, *Contemplative Prayer*, Darton, Longman & Todd: 1973

René Voillaume, *Faith and Contemplation*, Darton, Longman & Todd: 1974